1000 HOURS OUTSIDE™

Outdoor Cooking with Kids

Everything Tastes Better Outside

Ginny Yurich

1000 Hours Outside Outdoor Cooking With Kids
ISBN: 979-8-218-97168-7
Copyright @2024 by Ginny Yurich
Contributor: Meagan Nowacki of The Bluebirds Nest

Cover design and book layout by Saint Creative
www.saint-creative.com

Correspondence and comments?
Write to hello@1000hoursoutside.com

Eating outdoors makes for good health and long life and good temper, everyone knows that.

-Elsie De Wolfe

TABLE OF CONTENTS

Outdoor Cooking with Kids

INTRODUCTION

Everything Tastes Better Outside

It's hard to slow down. Life moves at a fast clip that only seems to get faster as our children get older. Cooking outside presses the pause button on life. It's similar to cooking inside, it just takes longer. So often in life, we avoid what takes longer. Why heat something over a stovetop when we have a microwave? Why pop popcorn over a fire when we can get a perfect batch in just two minutes at the press of a button?

Why? Because a lot of life happens during the waiting.

So, hurry up and wait. Pack up your supplies. Do a little prep. Build your fire. Wait for it to get hot. Take a little extra time to make your meal and enjoy it out in the open air. If you can manage, bring a tablecloth because a simple tablecloth makes everything feel more festive.

Let's Begin

It's hard to try new things. There will be some failure. Cooking over a fire isn't a precise science. It's not like turning the oven to 450 degrees and watching through the glass window for the perfectly baked end result. There will be some trial and error here; this is the time to use your senses. If it smells like something is burning, take it off the flames. Check your cooking progress sooner rather than later. Even if things go wrong, it might not all be lost! Just scrape off that bottom charred layer and enjoy the top. You'll get the hang of this quickly, and it's worth attempting something new. Besides, you are modeling bravery and adaptability to your family and that's exciting!

How to Use This Book

We've included common recipes in this book that can be adapted to the outdoors. In most cases we've included photos of the ingredients because these would be perfect camping recipes. Packing up for camping trips takes a lot of forethought and these pictures should help with meal prep. Use these recipes here and there throughout your daily life. Use them for gatherings. Use them for weekend camping trips. Use them to help you rack up your 1000 Hours Outside!

Safety

We must always use the utmost caution when cooking over an open fire. Cast iron cookware adds an extra element to be aware of because it retains heat for a long period of time and also because it is fairly heavy. When working around open flames and hot coals, make sure to be mindful of children at all times and have everyone maintain a safe distance from the fire at all times. In addition, be extremely careful when moving heavy dutch ovens or cast-iron skillets, opening dutch oven lids (watch for steam), and even once you are finished cooking, be sure no one brushes up against your cookware before it has cooled down. If you have little ones around, verify that you have enough help before embarking on cooking over a fire. Take your time. Move slowly. Check and double check your surroundings. Don't continue if you feel safety has been compromised.

Equipment

For the recipes that follow we use two main pieces of cookware: a cast-iron skillet and a cast-iron Dutch oven. The main skillet we used was 15-inch in diameter and the Dutch oven we used held 12L. Choose your cookware depending on the size of the crowd you are feeding.

We also regularly used long metal tongs, a long metal spoon with a wooden handle, heat and fire resistant gloves, heavy-duty aluminum foil, and cooking spray.

For Parents, Teachers and Caregivers

Many of the recipes that follow are perfect for including kids! Depending on their ages they can crack eggs, line your Dutch oven with sliced bread, cut up small cubes of cream cheese, fill their quesadillas and so much more!

BREAKFAST

"ALL HAPPINESS DEPENDS ON A LEISURELY BREAKFAST." – JOHN GUNTHER

Each new day arises with hope and expectation. So often when we wake up our minds are already reeling with a long checklist of to-dos. Responsibilities can weigh us down but if we can sneak in a breakfast outdoors, eating in the open air and allowing full-spectrum sunlight to permeate our eyes and our skin, we can set ourselves and our families on a beautiful path for the remainder of the day. Morning sunlight travels right to our brains and helps our bodies release serotonin, a feel good chemical. Use these recipes on the weekends, while camping, or even on a weekday morning if you can squeeze it in! You might be a little tired at first, but starting off a day in nature is invigorating.

French Toast

It couldn't be simpler! Sliced bread and beaten eggs make up this favorite dish. There are all sorts of variations to make this one your own. Depending on your time frame you can make your breakfast French toast more like a casserole or you can fry it up in a skillet. Either way, you'll have some happy kids.

Dutch Oven French Toast

TIME: 15 minutes to prepare, 35 minutes to cook
Feeds four to six

INGREDIENTS:

*1 one-pound loaf of French or Italian bread sliced into strips or torn into pieces

*12-14 eggs

*1 8 oz. package of cream cheese, cut into 1 cm. cubes

*2 Tablespoons ground cinnamon

*1 Tablespoon vanilla extract

TOPPINGS (optional):

*1 can of diced peaches

*½ cup powdered sugar

*8 oz. maple syrup

Also needed: aluminum foil and a can of cooking spray

COOKING INSTRUCTIONS:

1. Line your dutch oven with your aluminum foil and coat the foil with cooking spray.

2. Whisk eggs in a mixing bowl.

3. Add cinnamon to the eggs.

4. Add vanilla extract to eggs.

5. Take your strips or pieces of bread and lay them along the bottom of the dutch oven.

6. Spread out all of your cubes of cream cheese evenly across the strips of bread.

7. Add one more set of bread strips or pieces on top of the cream cheese.

8. Pour your egg mixture over everything.

9. Bake for about 30 - 35 minutes making sure you have coals covering the top of your dutch oven lid as well as coals underneath. You'll know it's done when the cream cheese has melted.

10. Serve plain or with toppings.

French Toast

It couldn't be simpler! Sliced bread and beaten eggs make up this favorite dish. There are all sorts of variations to make this one your own. Depending on your time frame you can make your breakfast French toast more like a casserole or you can fry it up in a skillet. Either way, you'll have some happy kids.

Skillet Corn Flakes French Toast

TIME: 5 minutes to prepare, 10 minutes to cook
Feeds five to six

INGREDIENTS:

*1 loaf of sliced bread, about 12 pieces

*6 eggs

*1 teaspoon vanilla extract.

*2 Tablespoons butter

*4 cups of crushed cornflakes cereal

TOPPINGS (optional):

*½ cup powdered sugar

*8 oz. maple syrup

COOKING INSTRUCTIONS:

1. Whisk eggs in a mixing bowl.

2. Add vanilla extract.

3. Melt butter in a skillet over the fire.

4. Dip both sides of a slice of bread in the egg mixture, then dip both sides in the cornflakes.

5. Fry one side of your bread until browned for about four to five minutes then flip and fry the other side.

6. Continue the same process with your remaining slices of bread.

7. Serve with toppings if desired.

"Griddle cakes, pancakes, hot cakes, flapjacks: why are there four names for grilled batter and only one word for love?"
-George Carlin

7.

8.

Flapjacks

Pile 'em up high! Prepare your toppings! Flapjacks are fun because they can be completely customized. Make your flapjacks from scratch or choose a quicker route by using a prepared muffin mix. When making your recipe from scratch, you can prepare all of your dry ingredients ahead of time and store them in a plastic zippered bag or in a glass jar with a lid. When it's time for breakfast, just add in the wet ingredients, stir, and get to flipping.

Skillet Flapjacks with Topping Bar

TIME: 15 minutes to prepare batter, 20 minutes to cook

INGREDIENTS:

Dry ingredients (can be mixed ahead prior)

*2 cups flour

*2 Tablespoons sugar

*2 teaspoons baking powder

*1 teaspoon baking soda

*1 teaspoon salt

Wet ingredients:

*2 cups milk

*2 eggs

*1 teaspoon vanilla

Also needed: a stick of butter or a can of cooking spray

Optional toppings: cut-up strawberries, cut-up apples, cut-up peach bites, blueberries, raspberries, thin banana slices, thin kiwi slices, pecans, chocolate chips, whipped cream, confectioners sugar, maple syrup or camp syrup.

COOKING INSTRUCTIONS:

1. Prepare your fire ahead of time so that you'll have a hot bed of coals ready.

2. Mix dry ingredients together and stir.

3. Mix wet ingredients together and stir.

4. Mix wet ingredients into dry ingredients and stir until smooth. Add slightly more flour for thicker batter or slightly more milk or water for thinner batter.

5. Spray your cast-iron skillet with cooking spray or grease with butter.

6. Place your cast-iron skillet on a grate over your bed of coals or set it directly on the coals.

7. Pour about ½ cup of batter into the greased skillet. Once the top of the flapjack begins to make little bubbles you can add your toppings or wait to put them on top once your flapjack is fully cooked. 8. Flip your flapjack and brown the other side. 9. Repeat the process until you have a huge pile of flapjacks. Add toppings and enjoy!

Skillet Muffin Mix Flapjacks Variation

Follow the same cooking instructions as above but make the process easier with muffin mix. Choose a favorite flavor like wild blueberry or apple cinnamon. Mix a 7 ounce package of muffin mix with one egg and ⅓ cup of water, stir well and your mix is ready to go!

Dutch Oven Cheesy Ham and Potato Breakfast Casserole

This one is sure to please a crowd! Watch out because they'll be wandering your way as soon as the alluring aroma of the casserole begins to waft through the air. These are hearty enough to be used for other meals than breakfast but on a chilly morning, a warm meal is one of the best things you can have!

TIME: 10 minutes to prepare, 20 minutes to cook
Feeds four to six

INGREDIENTS: [CB_007]

*32 oz. diced frozen hash brown potatoes

*8 oz. cooked, diced ham

*16 oz. sour cream

*2 cups shredded sharp cheddar cheese

*1 small onion, chopped

*2 10.75 oz. cans of cream of potato soup (if you can't find cream of potato soup you can use cream of celery instead)

Also needed: Aluminum foil, cooking spray

COOKING INSTRUCTIONS:

1. Prepare your fire ahead of time so that you'll have a hot bed of coals ready.

2. Once you have a hot bed of coals, place your dutch oven with the lid on over your coals and preheat it for 15 minutes.

3. Carefully add a layer of aluminum foil to your dutch oven and spray with cooking spray.

4. Dump all the ingredients in your dutch oven and give it a stir.

5. Place the lid back on the oven and return it to the coals. Leave at least 10 coals underneath the dutch oven, making sure they aren't touching the oven and place 15 - 20 pieces of charcoal on the lid.

6. Let your casserole cook for 30 minutes.

7. Carefully remove the lid and voila! Your piping hot breakfast is served!

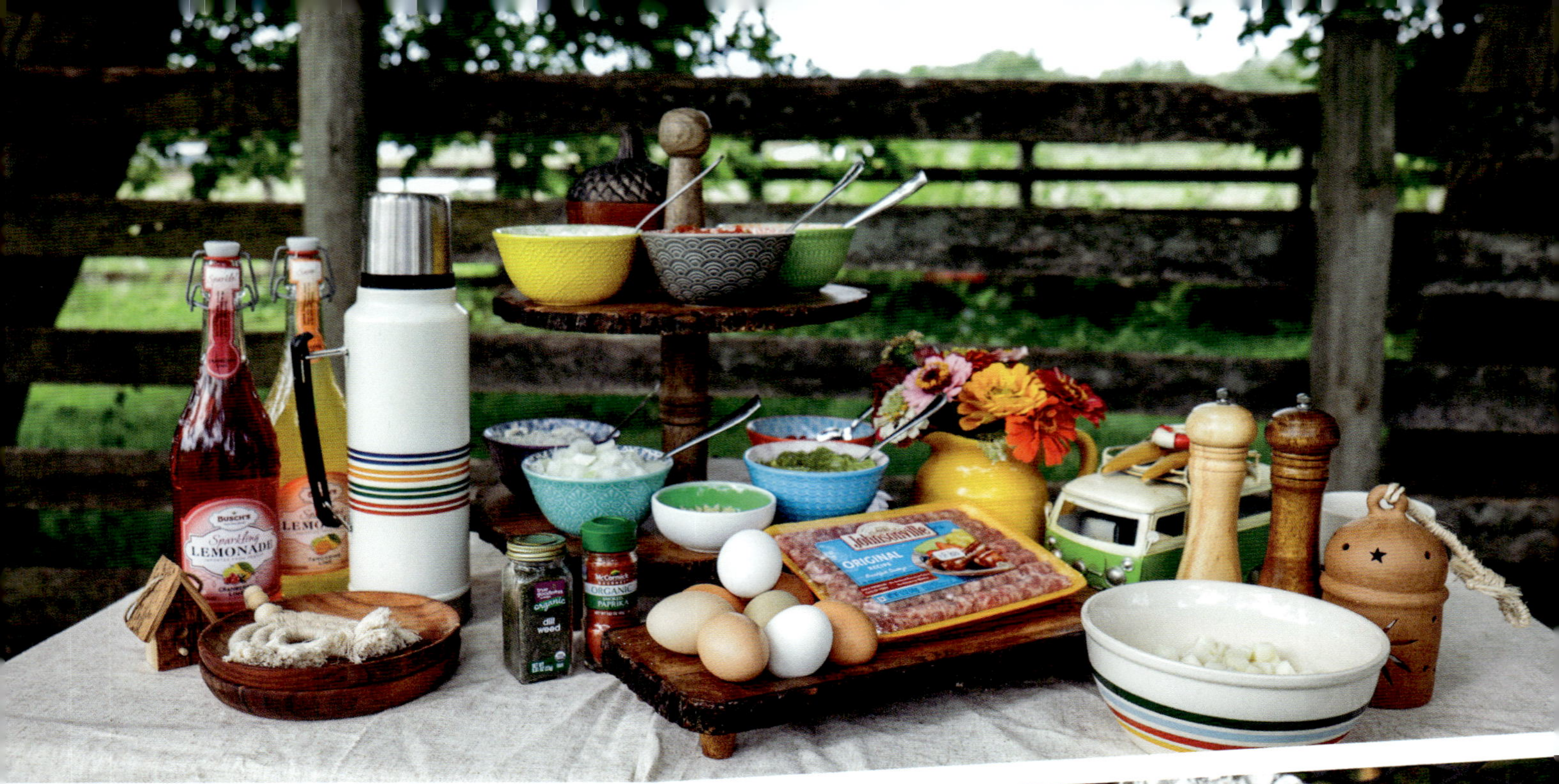
BUSCH'S
Sparkling
LEMONADE
Johnsonville
ORIGINAL
dill weed
ORGANIC
PAPRIKA

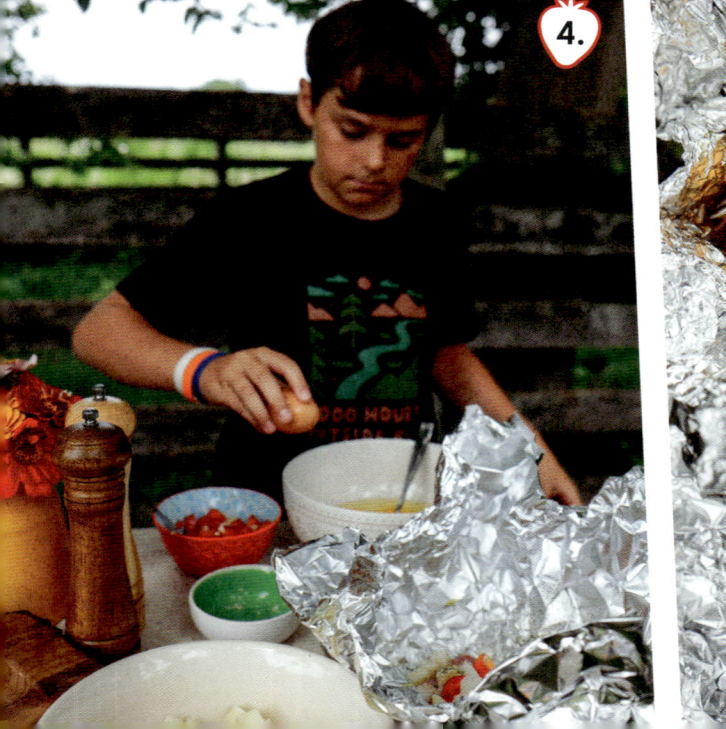

4.

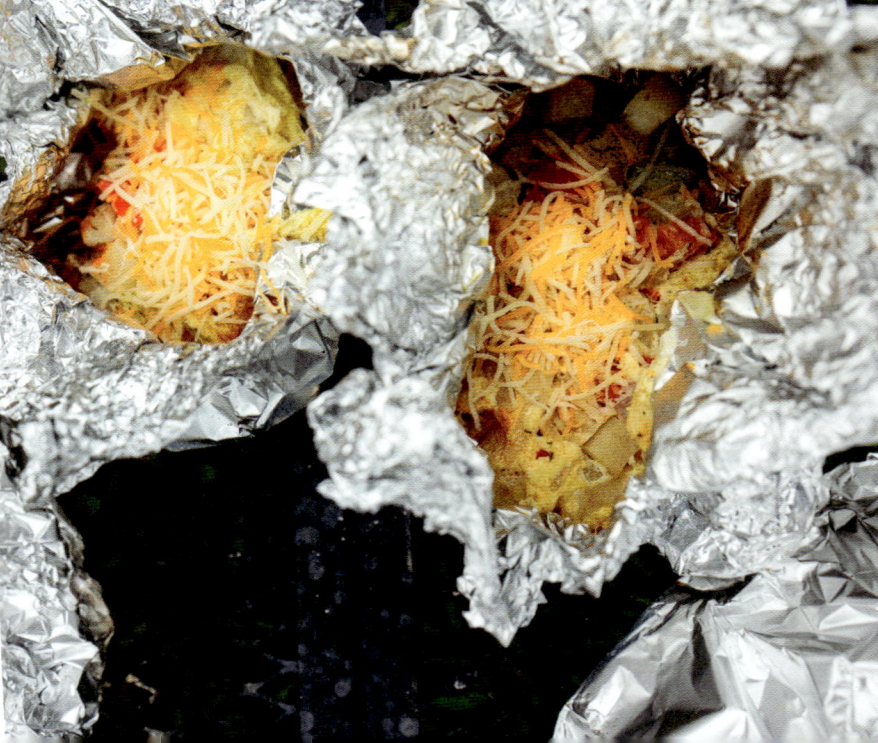

Foil Breakfast Pouches

This breakfast is a lot of fun for everyone to make. If you have picky eaters, this is a winner. No onions or peppers? No problem. These powerhouse pouches are totally customizable! Feel free to substitute or add any ingredients with ones that your family loves best. Don't forget to have seasonings available like dried dill, smoked paprika, or Italian seasoning. There's no wrong way to enjoy this custom camp favorite - Just don't forget the hot sauce!

Adventurer's Breakfast

TIME: 10 minutes to prepare, 20 minutes to cook
Feeds four

INGREDIENTS:

*8 eggs

*16 sausage links

*1 bag frozen hash browns (15 oz)

*1 cup diced bell peppers

*1 cup diced onions

*2 teaspoons minced garlic (pre-minced in the jar is great)

*1 bag colby jack cheese (8 oz)

*Salt and pepper to taste

Also needed: Aluminum foil, cooking spray
Optional Toppings: salsa, guacamole, spinach dip, hot sauce

COOKING INSTRUCTIONS:

1. Tear off 4 large squares of heavy duty tin foil and spray each one liberally with cooking spray or olive oil spray. Fold all of the edges slightly upward into a cup or bowl shape to hold the eggs when they are added.

2. Put 4 sausages in each piece of foil.

3. Add hash browns on top about ⅓ cup or a large handful and sprinkle on a little salt and pepper.

4. Mix minced garlic in with the peppers and add ¼ cup to each packet along with a ¼ cup of onions and 2 eggs. Sprinkle salt and pepper as well as any additional dry seasonings on top. [NEW_02]

5. Wrap up the packet and make sure each side is closed securely before double wrapping it in more foil.

6. Cook over the fire or on the grill for 15-20 minutes and make sure you turn it once halfway through cooking time. [NEW_04]

7. Open the pouches to make sure the sausage is cooked through. Continue cooking if needed. When sausage is done, add about 2 ounces of cheese to each pouch, close them up, and cook for another 5 minutes to melt the cheese.

8. Serve with toppings like salsa, guacamole, spinach dip, and of course hot sauce. Enjoy!

Foil Breakfast Pouches

This is a riff on the old classic "Eggy Toast" that we grew up eating at home. It goes by many names but basically it's a whole egg cooked inside of a piece of buttery, toasted bread with a hole cut into it. Adventure fuel needs to have just a little more substance so we've swapped the toast for a baked potato and added some parmesan cheese. This will definitely have you feeling sunny, regardless of the weather at camp!

TIME: 5 minutes to prepare, 60 - 70 minutes to cook
Feeds four

INGREDIENTS:

*4 baking potatoes

*1 stick softened butter

*4 eggs

*4 tablespoon grated parmesan cheese

*Seasoned salt and pepper to taste

Also needed: Aluminum foil, cooking spray

COOKING INSTRUCTIONS:

1. Scrub each potato well and coat completely with softened butter.

2. Wrap each potato tightly in heavy duty tin foil.

3. Place potatoes in the hot coals of the campfire for 45-60 minutes (depending on the size of your potatoes)

4. Remove from the heat and carefully unwrap.

5. Slice each potato down the middle but not all the way through to the bottom and open it up slightly. Spread more butter inside and sprinkle some seasoned salt and pepper to taste.

6. Break an egg into the opening and add the parmesan cheese.

7. Rewrap in foil and return to the coals "egg side up" and bake until egg is set.
(approximately 5-7 minutes)

6.

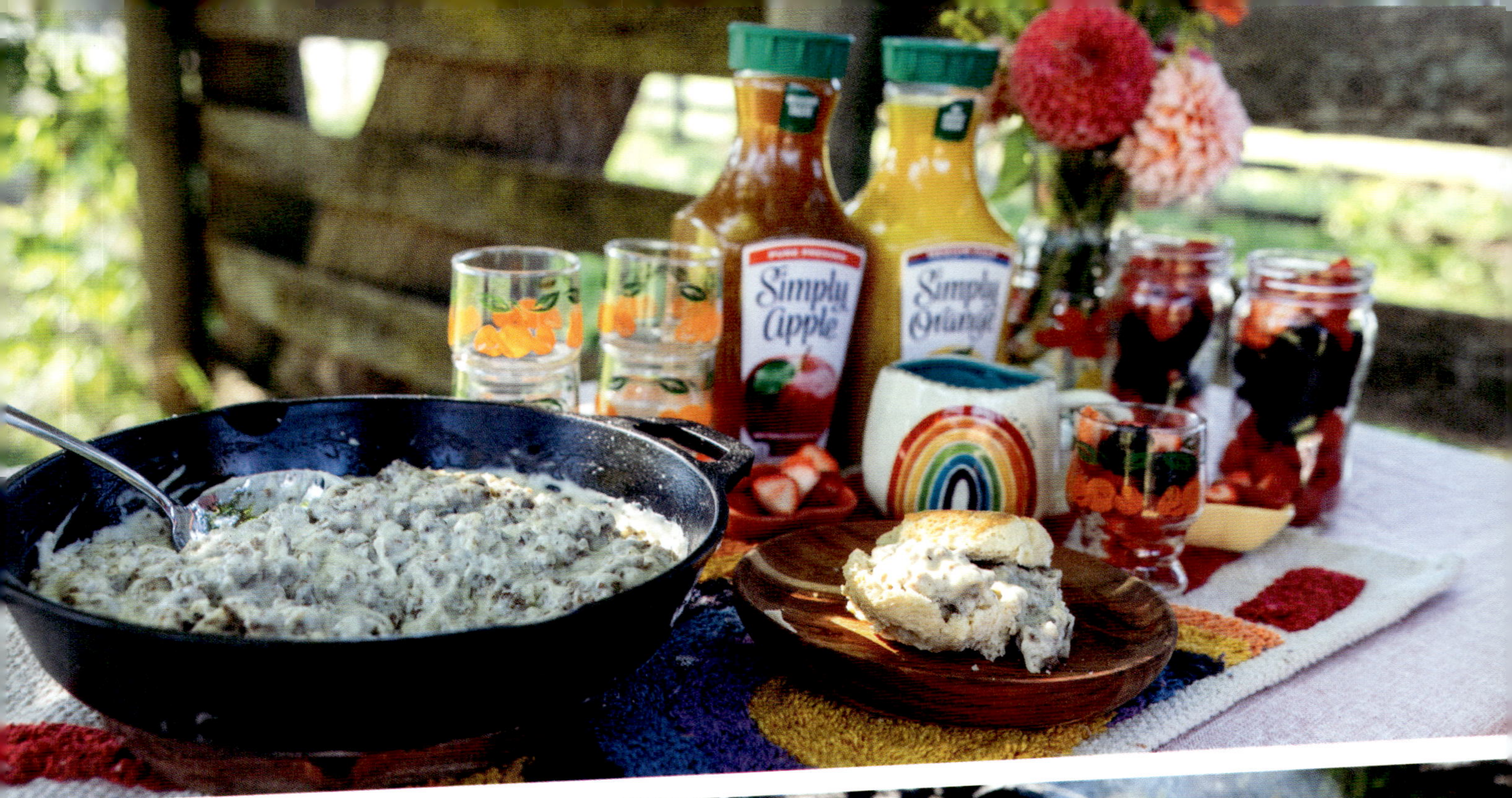
Simply Apple
Simply Orange

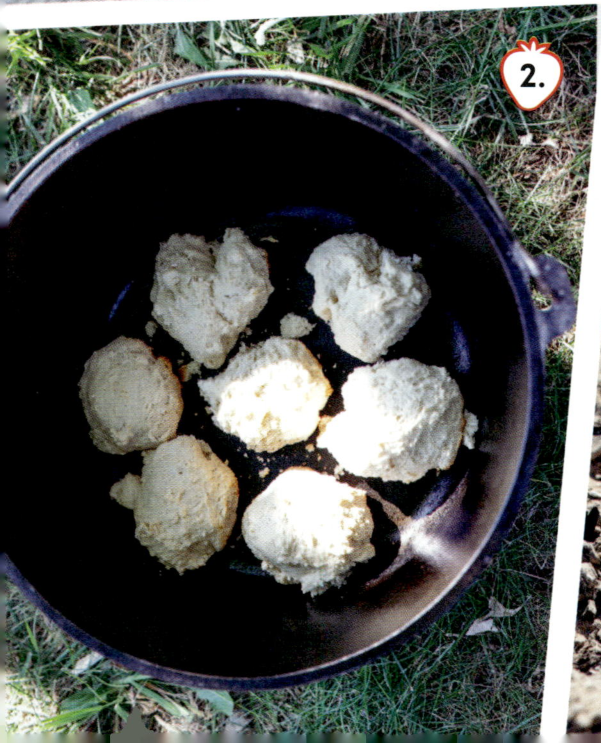
2.

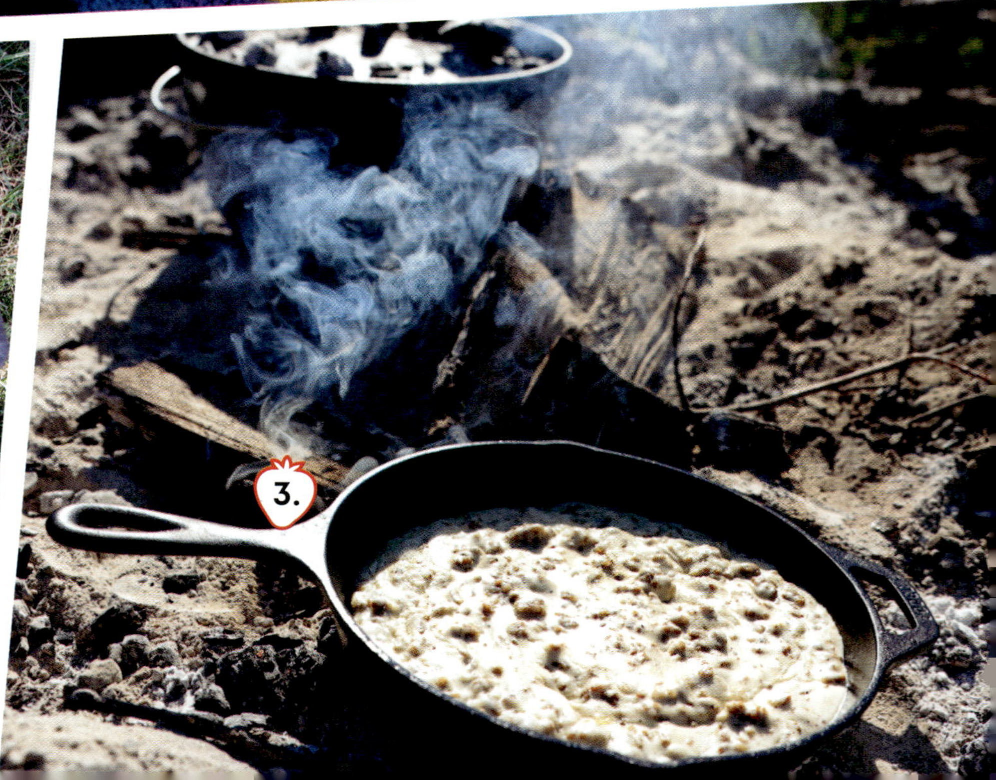
3.

Bigfoot's Biscuits and Gravy

We all know the campfire lore about that towering, hairy, and chronically shy giant who inhabits the woods. We've never been able to ask him what his favorite breakfast is but I have it on good authority it's these delicious biscuits with a hearty helping of sausage gravy. Don't ask me how I know this…I promised not to tell. When you're as hungry as a sasquatch, look no further than this BIG favorite!

TIME: 15 minutes to prepare, 25-30 minutes to cook
Feeds four to six

INGREDIENTS:
For the biscuits:

*2 ¼ cup Bisquick Baking Mix

*⅔ cup whole milk

For the gravy:

*1 pound breakfast sausage (spicy or mild will work or you can use turkey sausage)

*2-3 tablespoons butter (you may not need all of this - see note)

*¼ cup flour

*3 cups whole milk

*Salt and pepper to taste

Also needed: Cooking spray

COOKING INSTRUCTIONS:
1. In a mixing bowl or gallon sized plastic bag, combine the Bisquick and milk. Mix with a spoon or knead in the bag to combine. Set aside.

2. Grease your dutch oven well and then form 8 biscuits from your dough mixture about ¾ of an inch thick and about 2 inches in diameter. Arrange them in the bottom of your oven.

3. Bake the biscuits using 8 briquettes underneath the oven and 17 coals on the top of the lid. Cook until biscuits are lightly golden brown and risen (about 20-25 minutes)

4. While the biscuits are baking, prepare the gravy by cooking the sausage until golden brown in a hot skillet. Add the butter if necessary and then add the flour. Stir the flour in well and cook it for 1-2 minutes.

5. Add the milk and stir until thickened making sure to scrape up the brown bits at the bottom of the skillet. Taste for salt and add some if necessary. Add a generous amount of black pepper.

6. Crumble each biscuit or cut them in half and serve with sausage gravy on top.

*Note: You want at least 3 tablespoons of fat in the pan before adding the flour. If you don't have much fat, then add the whole 3 tablespoons. You may need to add less or none at all. Just judge it by eye and add accordingly.

4.

Scrambled Clouds

This easy, cheesy scramble is packed full of protein so you can hit the trails with plenty of energy. Even if you think you don't like cottage cheese, give this a chance and just see. The mix of eggs and cheese becomes light and bright and fluffy… just like the clouds you'll see on your hike!

TIME: 5 minutes to prepare, 10 minutes to cook
Feeds four

INGREDIENTS:

*4 tablespoons butter

*6 eggs

*4 tablespoons whole milk

*1 ⅓ cup cottage cheese

*⅔ cup shredded monterey jack cheese

*1 teaspoon onion powder

*1 teaspoon garlic powder

*Salt and pepper to taste

COOKING INSTRUCTIONS:

1. Melt butter in a large pan over low heat.

2. While butter is melting, whisk eggs and milk in a large bowl until well combined and slightly frothy. Add the garlic and onion powder as well as some salt and pepper.

3. Add the cottage cheese to the pan and spread it out evenly. Let this simmer over low heat for about 2 minutes and then add the grated cheese and stir together.

4. When the cheese mixture comes back to a simmer, add the eggs to the pan and using a spatula, fold the mixture together by turning it over gently constantly until set.

5. Once set, taste for seasonings and serve with buttered toast.

3.

4.

2.

4.

5.

Breakfast Sandwiches

Here is a mash up of two absolute classics: french toast and a peanut butter sandwich! This is a real crowd pleaser and a great way to start the day. You'll love how fast this breakfast comes together and I guarantee you'll be leftover free. If you're feeling creative, how about some add-ins like chocolate chips, sliced bananas, or even some crunchy granola? Whatever you decide, this will definitely be the perfect peanut butter breakfast sandwich!

Perfect Peanut Butter Breakfast Sandwich

TIME: 10 minutes to prepare, 10-15 minutes to cook
Feeds six

INGREDIENTS:

*6 eggs

*1 teaspoon vanilla extract

*1 teaspoon cinnamon

*1 cup whole milk

*12 slices bread

*1 cup peanut butter

*Butter for greasing skillet or griddle

*Maple syrup and powdered sugar for serving

Optional extras: Chocolate chips, sliced bananas, granola

COOKING INSTRUCTIONS:

1. In a large bowl, whisk together the eggs, milk, vanilla, and cinnamon. Set aside.

2. Make 6 peanut butter sandwiches. Leave them plain or add extras.

3. Melt butter in your hot skillet or griddle.

4. Dip each sandwich in the custard mixture and cook over medium high heat until golden.

5. Serve with syrup and powdered sugar.

Breakfast Sandwiches

This breakfast sandwich is quick, portable, and full of familiar flavors. I think eating this while taking in the scenic natural views of the forest beats the golden arches any day. Enjoy!

Egg McStuffin

TIME: 10 minutes to prepare, 10 minutes to cook
Feeds six

INGREDIENTS:

*6 English muffins

*6 eggs

*2 tablespoons milk or half and half

*6 slices canadian bacon

*6 slices American cheese

*Softened butter

*Salt and pepper

COOKING INSTRUCTIONS:

1. In a large mixing bowl whisk together the eggs, milk, and salt and pepper until slightly frothy.

2. Heat your skillet and melt about 2 tablespoons of butter. Add the Canadian bacon and cook until lightly browned on both sides. Set Aside.

3. Add a little more butter and toast halved english muffins (cut side down) until lightly crisped and golden. Set Aside.

4. Turn the heat down to low and add the eggs to the pan. Using a spatula, fold the eggs over gently constantly until set.

5. To each sandwich, add a cheese slice on the bottom followed by a sixth of the eggs, and then the canadian bacon.

6. Serve immediately or wrap in foil to eat on the go.

Breakfast Burritos

These hearty burritos turn camp breakfast into a real fiesta! The spicy chorizo is the real star of this dish and it will warm you up from the inside out. Serve these up with sour cream, salsa, and guacamole, and you'll be hearing "Gracias!"

Backpacker's Breakfast Burritos

TIME: 10 minutes to prepare, 15 minutes to cook
Feeds eight

INGREDIENTS:

*Pre-cooked Chorizo Sausage (14 oz) cut into small pieces

*12 eggs

*2 tablespoons butter

*1 bag (20 oz) "Ore-Ida Potatoes O'Brien" (hash browns w/peppers & onions)

*8 oz Mexican Blend Cheese with taco seasoning

*8 flour tortillas (burrito size)

*Salt and pepper to taste

COOKING INSTRUCTIONS:

1. In a large bowl whisk eggs to break up and combine. Add salt and pepper.

2. Melt butter in a large skillet over medium heat and add chopped chorizo.

3. Once the chorizo is browned, add the eggs and the hash browns and scrabble until the eggs are cooked.

4. Add cheese and stir until melted and well combined. Taste for seasoning and add more salt and pepper as needed.

5. On each tortilla, place about ¾ cup of the mixture. Roll up and serve with toppings or put toppings inside and wrap in foil to take on the go.

Breakfast Burritos

These breakfast burritos are perfect if you have a vegetarian in your crew or if you're looking for a way to add more plant based protein to your own diet. Black beans and sweet potatoes will keep you going for hours whether you're outside enjoying nature or having a busy day at work or home. These are made ahead at home and stored in the refrigerator until ready to transfer to a cooler. This time saving breakfast will make for some very happy campers!

Make Ahead Veggie Breakfast Burritos

TIME: 35 minutes to prepare, 10 minutes to cook
Feeds six

INGREDIENTS:
*2 sweet potatoes (diced and roasted *see note) or 1 (10 oz) bag frozen chopped sweet potatoes
*3 tablespoons olive oil or avocado oil
*1 teaspoon ground cumin
*1 teaspoon garlic powder
*½ teaspoon dried chili powder
*6 eggs beaten
*2 tablespoons whole milk
*12 tablespoons sour cream
*1 (15 oz) can black beans drained (pinto beans will also work)
*6 whole wheat tortillas (burrito size)
*2 cups shredded cheese of choice (pepper jack is great)
*Salt and pepper to taste

COOKING INSTRUCTIONS:
1. Heat oven to 400

2. Peel and dice sweet potatoes into ¼ inch pieces. In a bowl, toss the potatoes with 2 tablespoons of oil, cumin, garlic powder, chili powder, and a generous sprinkle of salt and pepper.

3. On a sheet pan, roast the potatoes for 20 minutes or until golden and tender.

4. Drain and rinse the black beans and season with a little salt and pepper. Set aside.

5. Heat a large skillet on your stovetop and add 1 tablespoon of oil.

6. In a large bowl, whisk the eggs and milk and add salt and pepper. Add the eggs to the skillet and using a spatula, fold the eggs over gently and constantly until set.

7. Add the black beans to the eggs and toss gently to combine. Remove from the heat and let the eggs sit while you prepare the tortillas.

8. Spread 2 tablespoons of sour cream on each tortilla, next add the eggs and bean mixture followed by sweet potatoes and cheese.

9. Fold the bottom of the tortilla upward and then roll up from one side keeping the bottom section folded upward to contain the contents on that end.

10. Double wrap each burrito in foil and store in the fridge until ready to serve. These can be warmed up in the coals of the fire or in a skillet. Turn often.

9.

3.

Blue Ridge Mountains Blueberry Coffee Cake

Yes! You can bake a cake over a campfire! This is a lovely breakfast treat on a crisp autumn morning at the campsite. The whole family will enjoy the aroma of sweet cinnamon wafting through the air and you'll feel right at home enjoying thick slices by the crackling morning fire. Where there's a whisk, there's a way so let's get baking!

TIME: 15 minutes to prepare, 30 minutes to cook
Feeds six to eight

INGREDIENTS:

*2 ¼ cup flour divided (hold back the ¼ cup and place it in a separate bowl)

*½ teaspoon salt

*1 tablespoon cinnamon

*1 cup brown sugar

*¾ cup granulated sugar

*¾ cup vegetable oil (or your favorite flavorless oil)

*1 teaspoon baking soda

*1 teaspoon baking powder

*1 egg

*1 teaspoon vanilla extract

*1 cup buttermilk

*1 ½ cups fresh blueberries

*1 cup chopped walnuts (you can use pecans instead if you prefer)

COOKING INSTRUCTIONS:

1. Line the bottom and sides of a 12" dutch oven with heavy duty tin foil and grease it well with nonstick spray

2. Preheat the oven using 8 coals underneath and 17 briquettes on the lid

3. In a large mixing bowl combine all ingredients except the blueberries and the chopped nuts.

4. Take the blueberries and toss them with the ¼ cup flour that you held back. Using a spatula, gently fold the blueberries into the batter. The flour will help the berries not to sink to the bottom of the cake.

5. Pour the batter into the greased dutch oven and sprinkle the nuts on top. Return the oven to the same position and arrange it again with the same amount of coals. Bake for 30 minutes. Check that the cake springs back when you lightly touch the center. If the cake is not set, continue baking in 3-5 minute increments. Enjoy!

LUNCH

"WHEN YOU'RE DOWN ON YOUR LUCK AND YOU'VE LOST ALL YOUR DREAMS THERE'S NOTHING LIKE A CAMPFIRE AND A CAN OF BEANS."
-TOM WAITS

Outdoor eating midday gives us a chance to pull back the reins a little bit. As the day is barreling forward, stepping outside to cook a meal forces us to slow down and recalibrate. For a few moments, we can set aside the tasks that may weigh us down to focus on our surroundings and all the beauty that lies around us. We can reconnect with nature, with our family, and with ourselves in this simple way. It takes a little more planning and a little more work to move a mid-day meal outside, but you will gain focus and refreshment to carry you through the rest of the afternoon.

4.

9.

Dutch Oven Sandwich Roll-Ups

Hand off the work to someone else with DIY Sandwich roll-ups! Lay out all of your favorite sandwich fillings, pile them in, and roll it up like a sleeping bag. Add some sesame seeds or other topping before you bake these and they'll look even fancier. This outdoor meal has a quick turnaround and offers a lot of variety for those darling little picky eaters.

Pizza Roll-Ups

TIME: 10 minutes to prepare, 10 - 15 minutes to cook. Feeds four to six

INGREDIENTS: [CB_022]

*2 8-count packages of crescent rolls

*1 cup pizza sauce

*2 cups mozzarella cheese

*6 oz. pepperoni cut into small pieces

Optional: Any other small pizza toppings like olives or bits of ham. Sesame seeds or a seasoning blend such as Italian or an everything blend.

COOKING INSTRUCTIONS:

1. Prepare your fire ahead of time so that you'll have a hot bed of coals ready but don't preheat your dutch oven. The sandwich roll-ups have a tendency to burn on the bottom before they're fully cooked through so you want to make sure the bottom of your dutch oven isn't too hot when you start.

2. Open your crescent roll tube and roll out your eight triangles.

3. Fill each triangle beginning with a thin layer of sauce, then mozzarella cheese, then pepperoni.

4. Roll up your triangle working from the bigger side down to the point. [CB_023]

5. Once you have all eight finished, sprinkle your seasonings on top of each one if you'd like.

6. Gently place them into your dutch oven, put the lid on, and carefully place it over your coals.

7. Add 10 - 15 briquettes to the top of your dutch oven lid.

8. Monitor your roll-ups carefully. If the bottoms are cooking too fast, move your dutch oven off the direct heat but leave your briquettes on the lid.

9. Cook until your dough is lightly browned and fully cooked through. [CB_025]

10. Remove with a spatula and enjoy!

Ham & Cheese and Three-Cheese Variations:
Make it your own with different fillings. A slice of deli-ham and some shredded cheddar cheese turns into a hot ham and cheese roll-up. Fill your crescent roll with three varieties of cheese for a tasty variation. In fact, anything you can smash relatively flat would work in these! The crescent roll packs usually come with eight triangles to use which must be a sign that you should experiment here!

Dutch Oven Home on the Range Soup

This one couldn't be easier and the flavor couldn't be better! Plus, it's a warm and filling lunch. Our kids devour this soup and ask for this recipe often. It's an easy one to keep ingredients on hand and you can brown the ground beef ahead of time to make the process even quicker mid-day. Double the ingredients and you can feed a crowd!

TIME: 35 minutes
Feeds five to six

INGREDIENTS: [CB_027]

*2 pounds ground beef (can be browned and drained ahead of time)

*2 10-ounce cans diced tomatoes and green chiles

*2 15-ounce cans black, kidney, or pinto beans

*2 10½-ounce cans condensed vegetable soup

Optional: Crackers

COOKING INSTRUCTIONS:

1. Preheat the Dutch oven for about 10 minutes.

2. Brown the ground beef and drain the grease if you haven't already.

3. Add in tomatoes, beans, and vegetable soup. Stir.

4. Place the lid on the Dutch oven and cook for 15 - 20 minutes with coals on top and beneath until the soup is heated through thoroughly. [CB_030]

5. Serve with crackers. [CB_031]

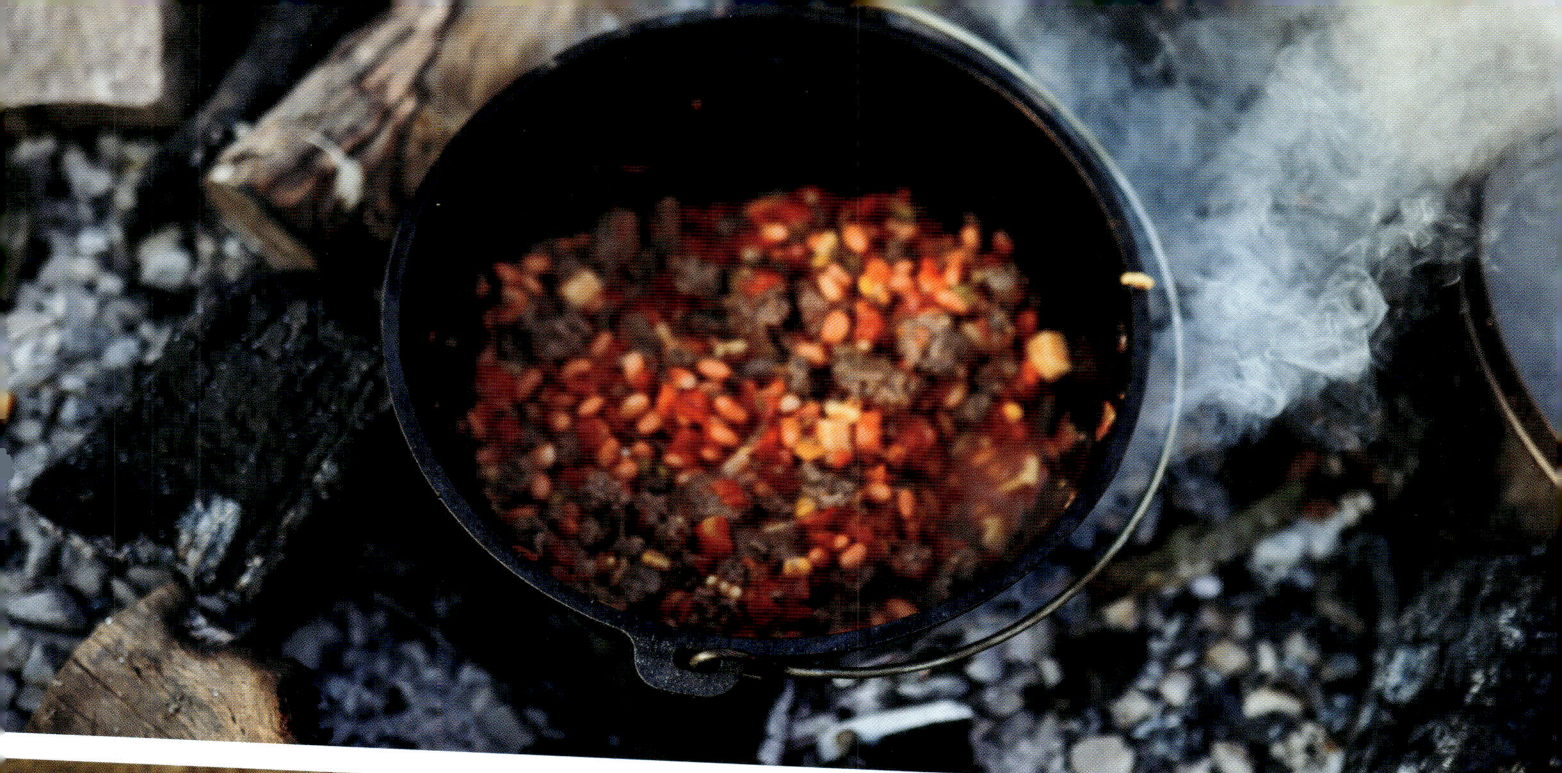

Campbell's
Vegetarian Vegetable Soup
Campbell's
Vegetarian Vegetable Soup
Hanover
Pinto Beans
Hanover
Pinto Beans
RO-TEL
Original
RO-TEL
Mild

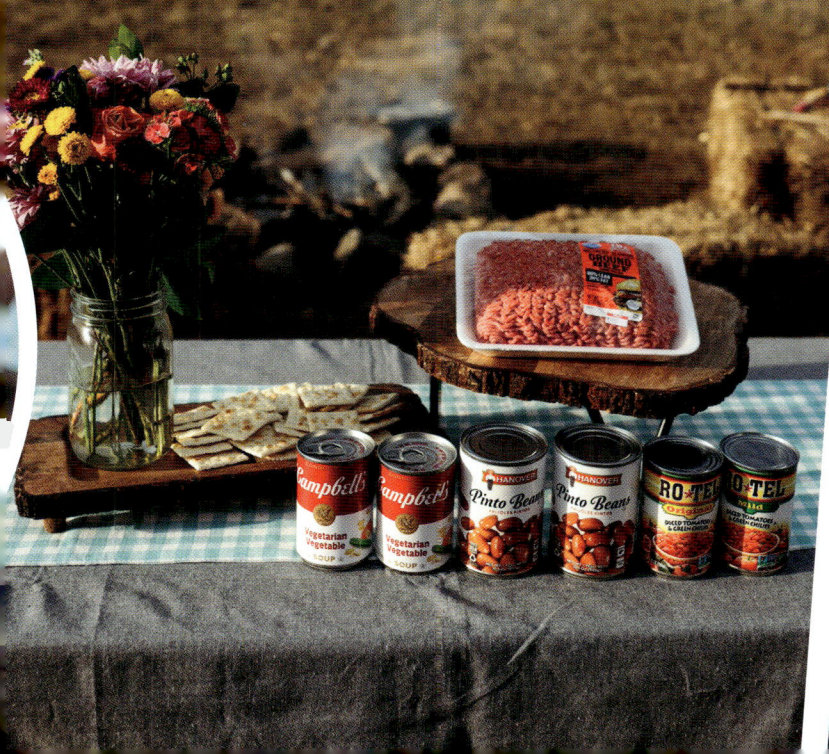

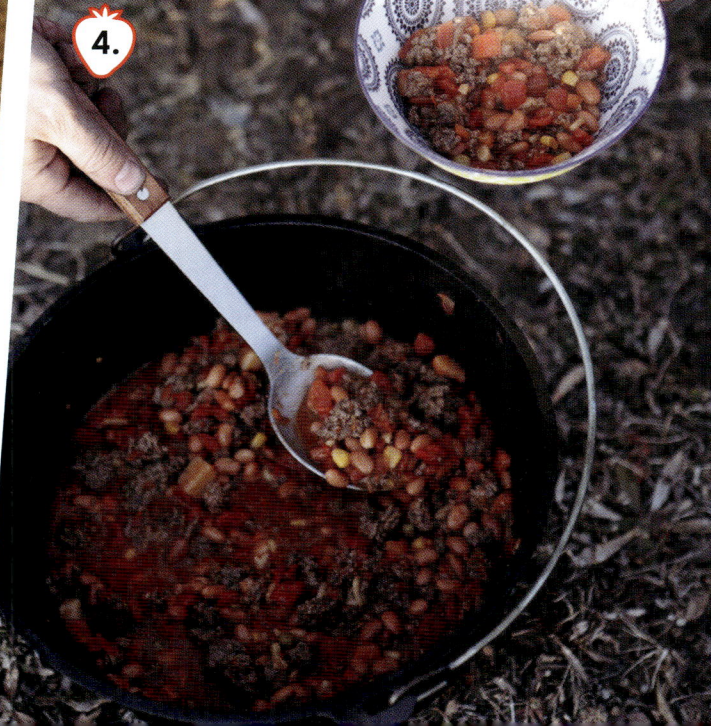

4.

3.

4.

5.

Foil Packet Quesadillas

These quesadillas cook up faster than you can whine, "I'm hungry." Well, maybe they take just a little bit longer but if you have kids who are ready for lunch, you can whip these up in no time. This is an easy recipe for kids to join in on, both to prepare the ingredients and to put them together.

TIME: 10 minutes to prepare, six to seven minutes to cook. Feeds four to six

INGREDIENTS:

*2 Tablespoons olive oil

*6 large 10-inch flour tortillas

*2 cups shredded cheese of your choice

FILLING OPTIONS:

*1 8.75-ounce can whole-kernel corn

*1 15-ounce can beans (black, pinto, or kidney)

*1 medium onion diced

*12 button mushrooms thinly sliced

*Colored peppers thinly sliced

TOPPING OPTIONS:

*Shredded lettuce

*Guacamole

*Salsa

*Sour cream

*Cilantro

Also needed: Aluminum foil

COOKING INSTRUCTIONS
(can be prepared ahead of time):

1. Heat the olive oil in a skillet and saute the mushrooms, onions, and peppers until tender. Add the corn and black beans and cook for three to five more minutes.

2. Let your mixture cool and put it in a sealed container, keeping it in the fridge until you are ready to use it.

3. To assemble your quesadillas, tear a piece of aluminum foil that's larger than your tortilla and place the tortilla on top. Do this for all of your tortillas.

4. Divide the cheese amongst all of your tortillas.

5. Spread your mushroom mixture on top of cheese.

6. Carefully fold the tortillas and foil in half and roll up all of the sides to seal it shut.

7. Place your foil packets on a grate over your fire or on the grate of a charcoal grill for about five to six minutes until the cheese is melted.

8. Add toppings and make some more!

6.

Grilled Sammies

Keep it simple for lunch by making a classic grilled cheese… with some upgrades! Italian style ham and cheese will have you living that dolce vita in the middle of the wilderness! A California style turkey club will like for sure make you say "Dude!" Enjoy!

Italian Style Ham and Cheese

TIME: 10 minutes to prepare, 15 - 20 minutes to cook
Feeds eights

INGREDIENTS:

*16 slices of bread

*16 slices mozzarella cheese

*16 slices smoked ham

*1 jar Italian roasted red peppers chopped

*1 teaspoon dried oregano

*1 stick softened salted butter

*8 tablespoons grated parmesan cheese

COOKING INSTRUCTIONS:

1. Drain the roasted peppers and chop into bite sized pieces. Sprinkle oregano over them and set aside.

2. To assemble the sandwiches, place one slice of mozzarella on the bottom, then add the ham, then some of the peppers, and then top with a second slice of mozzarella.

3. Generously butter the top slices of bread on each sandwich and sprinkle a tablespoon of parmesan cheese evenly over the bread pressing lightly to adhere.

4. Melt additional butter in your skillet and place the sandwich (unbuttered side down) in the skillet and toast for a minute or 2 being careful not to burn it.

5. Carefully flip the sandwich over and toast on the second side. You can eat this as is or heat up your favorite marinara sauce for dipping.

2.

3.

Grilled Sammies

Keep it simple for lunch by making a classic grilled cheese… with some upgrades! Italian style ham and cheese will have you living that dolce vita in the middle of the wilderness! A California style turkey club will like for sure make you say "Dude!" Enjoy!

California Turkey Club

TIME: 10 minutes to prepare, 15 - 20 minutes to cook
Feeds eights

INGREDIENTS:

*16 slices of bread

*16 slices pepper jack cheese

*16 slices smoked turkey

*1 pound cooked bacon (*see note)

*1 (8 oz) container guacamole

*1 stick salted softened butter

COOKING INSTRUCTIONS:

1. To assemble the sandwiches, place one slice of pepper jack cheese on the bottom, then the turkey, then a few slices of bacon, then some of the guacamole, and then the other slice of pepper jack.

2. Generously butter the tops of the sandwiches.

3. Add additional butter to the skillet and place the sandwich (unbuttered side down) into the skillet and toast 1-2 minutes being careful not to burn it.

4. Carefully flip it over and toast the other side.

*Note: The bacon for this recipe can be cooked in advance at home and stored in the fridge until ready to use. You can also cook extra bacon at breakfast and set aside until lunch. Another option is to use pre-cooked bacon in the package or bacon crumbles typically used in salads.

Waikiki Hot Dog Skewers

These easy little skewers are perfect for a quick lunch that everyone can be involved in. The beaches in Hawaii sure are beautiful but nothing will beat your very own little campsite when you make these! Serve them with easy sides like chips and cut up veggies. Aloha!

TIME: 5 minutes to prepare, 5 - 10 minutes to cook

INGREDIENTS:

*4-6 hotdogs cut into pieces

*1 (20 oz) can pineapple chunks (drained)

*1 bottle of your favorite barbecue sauce

COOKING INSTRUCTIONS:

1. Build a campfire.

2. Slide hotdog pieces and pineapple chunks on the long skewers or long pointed sticks. Brush the hotdogs with barbecue sauce.

3. Hold about 8 inches above hot coals until hotdogs are heated through and barbecue sauce and pineapple are caramelized.

2.

3.

3.

4.

2.

5.

Mountain Meatball Subs

A delicious hot lunch on a busy day of outdoor activity is a most welcome luxury. These subs take just a little time to put together but you'll hardly remember because the end result is so worth it. Savor the flavor of these hearty heroes and make magical meatball memories with the ones you love the most.

TIME: 20 minutes to prepare, 20 minutes to cook
Feeds four

INGREDIENTS:

*1 pound ground beef

*½ cup dry bread crumbs

*4 eggs beaten

*½ cup milk

*1 cup grated parmesan cheese divided (hold back ¼ cup)

*1 teaspoon salt

*½ teaspoon pepper

*2 teaspoons minced dehydrated onion

*1 teaspoon minced garlic (from the jar is great)

*2 teaspoons dried parsley

*1 teaspoon Italian seasoning

*3 tablespoons olive oil

*1 jar marinara sauce

*4 submarine sandwich buns

COOKING INSTRUCTIONS:

1. In a large bowl combine beef, bread crumbs, eggs, milk, ¾ cup parmesan cheese, salt, pepper, onion, garlic, parsley, and italian seasoning.

2. Mix well with your hands and form into 1 ½ inch meatballs.

3. In a large skillet, heat the olive oil and then brown the meatballs on both sides.

4. Pour over the jar of marinara sauce and fill up the empty jar about a third of the way full with water and add that to the skillet.

5. Bring to a simmer and cook the meatballs in the sauce for about 15-20 minutes until done.

6. Pile meatballs and sauce into buns and sprinkle with reserved parmesan cheese.

6.

Shepherd's Pie Burgers

For this lunch we are taking on the classic shepherd's pie but in burger form! These flavorful burgers are like cousins to Hobo Pies and neighbors to Sloppy Joes. You could say they're well connected! The potatoes are not mashed but they are cooked on top of the burgers with lots of other veggies inside of a foil packet. These may be quite the hybrid, but they are certainly a delicious variety!

TIME: 15 minutes to prepare, 20 - 30 minutes to cook
Feeds four

INGREDIENTS:

*1 pound ground beef

*1 medium potato sliced

*1 medium onion

*Optional veggies: Thinly sliced celery and carrots, bell peppers, cabbage, or zucchini

*Garlic powder

*Seasoned Salt

*Pepper

*4 hamburger buns

*Cheese slices

*Sliced tomato

*Lettuce

COOKING INSTRUCTIONS:

1. Season ground beef with seasoned salt and pepper. Form into 4 patties.

2. Place each patty on a separate piece of heavy duty aluminum foil.

3. Place slices of potato and onion on each patty along with any other optional veggies and season all with seasoned salt, garlic powder, and pepper.

4. Place another sheet of foil on top to form a triangle. Seal up the edges by folding them up together.

5. Place packets over coals or on a grill and cook until the internal temperature of the meat is 160 degrees and veggies are softened. Approximately 20-30 minutes.[LUNCH_20]

6. Use tongs to remove the packets. Place patties on the burger buns and top with cheese, lettuce, tomato and any other condiments you like. The veggies inside the packet can be eaten on top of the burgers or on the side. Enjoy!

5.

3.

1.

Pikes Peak Chicken Pot Pie

This is a hearty lunch for the hungry hoards that start descending upon the campsite around noon each day. Luckily, this pot pie is easy to put together and the result is absolutely delicious. The hardest part is waiting for it to bake and the easiest part is eating it! Enjoy!

California Turkey Club

TIME: 10 minutes to prepare, 40 minutes to cook
Feeds six

INGREDIENTS:

*2 (8 oz) cans crescent rolls

*4 tablespoons melted salted butter

*1 teaspoon garlic powder

*½ teaspoon dried parsley

*Salt and pepper

*2 cans (9 ¾ oz) chunk chicken drained

*1 (16 oz) container sour cream

*1 (15 oz) can mixed vegetables (peas and carrots) drained

*1 small chopped onion

*¼ cup grated parmesan cheese

*1 tablespoon cornmeal

COOKING INSTRUCTIONS:

1. Melt butter and add garlic powder and dried parsley to it. Grease a 12" Dutch oven liberally with cooking spray. Unroll one can of crescent roll dough and spread across the bottom. Spread half of the garlic butter on top of the dough.

2. Using 7 briquettes on the bottom and 16 coals on the lid, bake the bottom crust for 10 minutes. While the crust is baking, prepare the filling.

3. In a large bowl combine the sour cream, onion, and veggies. Season well with salt and pepper.

4. Remove the Dutch oven from the coals and spread the chicken mixture over it.

5. Unroll the second container of dough and place on top of the chicken mixture.

6. Spread the remaining garlic butter on top of the dough as well as the parmesan cheese and the cornmeal.

7. Return the Dutch oven to the same arrangement of coals and bake until golden brown. Approximately 30 minutes.

Cowboy's Pinto Pie

Beans have filled the bowls of cowboys for generations out on the range. These legendary legumes have been immortalized in song and poetry. Johnny Cash wrote a song about beans and we all know how the old rhyme goes… "beans, beans the magical fruit! The more you eat, the more you…" Well… The ending escapes me right now but try this pinto pie and you might remember the rest!

TIME: 10 minutes to prepare, 15 minutes to cook
Feeds six

INGREDIENTS:

*1 tablespoon olive oil

*1 large onion diced

*1 green bell pepper diced

*2 teaspoons minced garlic (from the jar is fine)

*2 cans (14 oz) pinto beans drained

*1 packet taco seasoning mix

*¾ cup water

*½ cup salsa

*1 (10 oz bag) Fritos corn chips

*8 oz. Shredded Cheese with taco seasonings

COOKING INSTRUCTIONS:

1. Preheat a 12" Dutch Oven using 23 charcoal briquettes under it.

2. Put the olive oil in the pan and saute the onion and pepper until softened and slightly browned.

3. Add in the pinto beans and the garlic. With a wooden spoon, mix the beans into the veggies and mash some of them a bit.

4. In a small bowl, mix together the taco seasoning and the water. Pour this into the bean mixture. Stir to combine.

5. Remove from the heat and mix in the salsa. Put the fritos and cheese on top in alternating layers. Place the lid back on and let this stand until the cheese is melted.

Optional toppings include shredded lettuce, sour cream, jalapenos, and sliced black olives.

DINNER

DINNER

"Cooking and eating food outdoors makes it taste infinitely better than the same meal prepared and consumed indoors."
- Fennel Hudson

The changes in the color spectrum of the day are meant to guide our bodies. There's something about being outside as the sky begins to change to the blues and purples, signaling to our bodies that it's time to slow down. Ending your day with a meal outdoors, is like wrapping a pretty bow on a present. It's the finishing touch that adds more than you would expect.

Dutch Oven Campground Nachos

Recipes that you can make your own are so perfect for families. This is a quick recipe that allows for lots of personalization and can easily be scaled up or down to feed a crowd or a small group. You could invite a few neighbors over on a weeknight for nachos over the fire. This is one of those recipes you can even eat with your hands. Lay it all out on a long cutting board down the middle of your picnic table and dig in!

TIME: 10 minutes to prepare, 15 minutes to cook
Feeds four to five

INGREDIENTS:
*1 12-ounce bag of tortilla chips
*1 15-ounce can of black beans, drained and rinsed
*1 4-ounce can of green chiles
*1 14.5-ounce can of fire-roasted tomatoes
*1 3.8-ounce can of sliced black olives
*1 avocado diced into bite size pieces
*3 cups shredded cheese, cheddar or Mexican-blend
*3 green onions, diced
*1 lime, cut in half
*½ cup fresh cilantro, chopped
*3 cups ground beef, cooked ahead of time (optional)

Topping options:
*Sour cream
*Salsa
*Hot sauce

Also needed: Aluminum foil

COOKING INSTRUCTIONS:

1. Line your dutch oven with aluminum foil.

2. This recipe is all about layering. Start with a layer of tortilla chips then add a bit of everything else except for the cilantro. Make sure you have drained your beans extremely well. If there is a lot of extra liquid, your nachos will be a little soggy.

3. Repeat all of the layers one or two more times and then top with any remaining cheese and sprinkle with cilantro.

4. Place the lid on the Dutch oven and cook for about 15 minutes until the cheese is melted, with some coals on top and below your Dutch oven.

5. Spread out your nachos, add toppings and a few squirts of lime juice.

Foil Packet Variation:
You can make the same recipe individually by making a packet out of a large sheet of aluminum foil. Spread out a large rectangle of aluminum foil. Place a handful of chips at the bottom and then add in your favorite ingredients and top with cheese. Fold the foil up over the top and at the edge to completely seal the edges. Place your packet in the hot coals for five to ten minutes or until the cheese is melted. Use caution when opening your packet to allow steam to escape. You can add your toppings right into your foil packet and have less mess to clean up afterwards!

5.

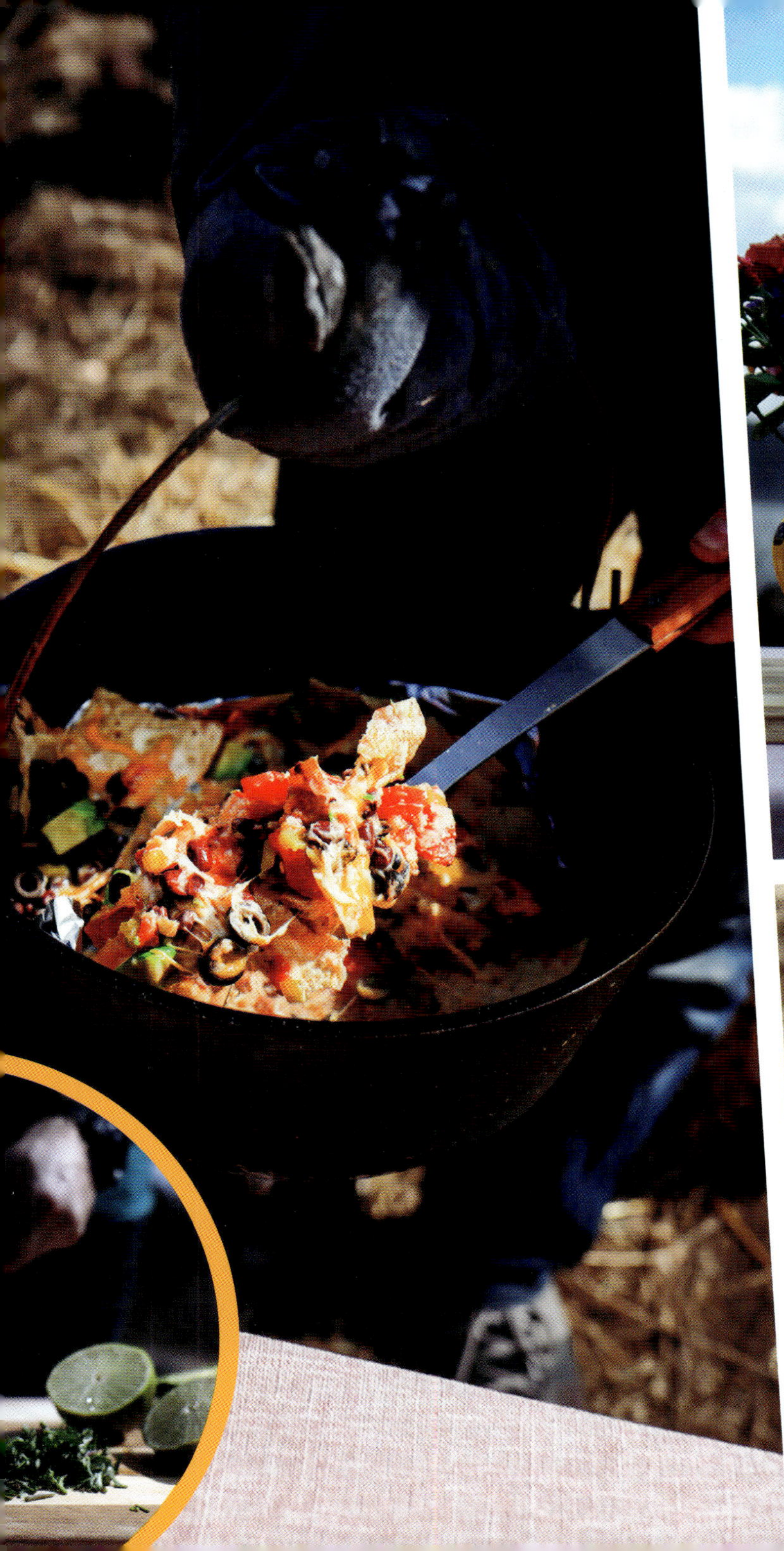

MEXICAN
STYLE BLEND
SHREDDED CHEESE
ORIGINAL
CILANTRO
Hunts
Diced

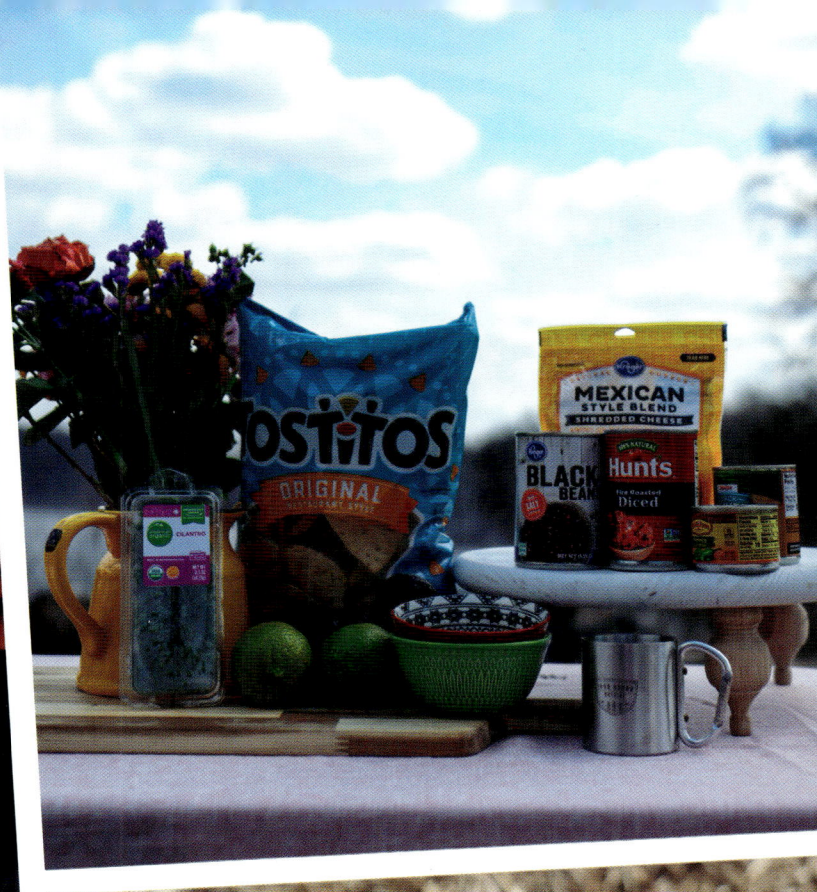

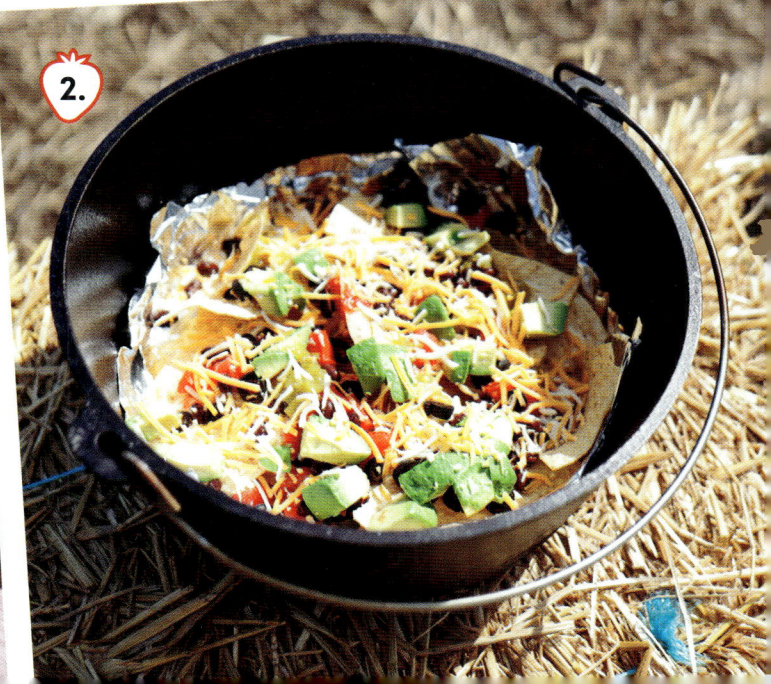

2.

Naturally
APPLEWOOD SMOKED
BACON
Daisy
SOUR CREAM
Daisy
SOUR
CREAM

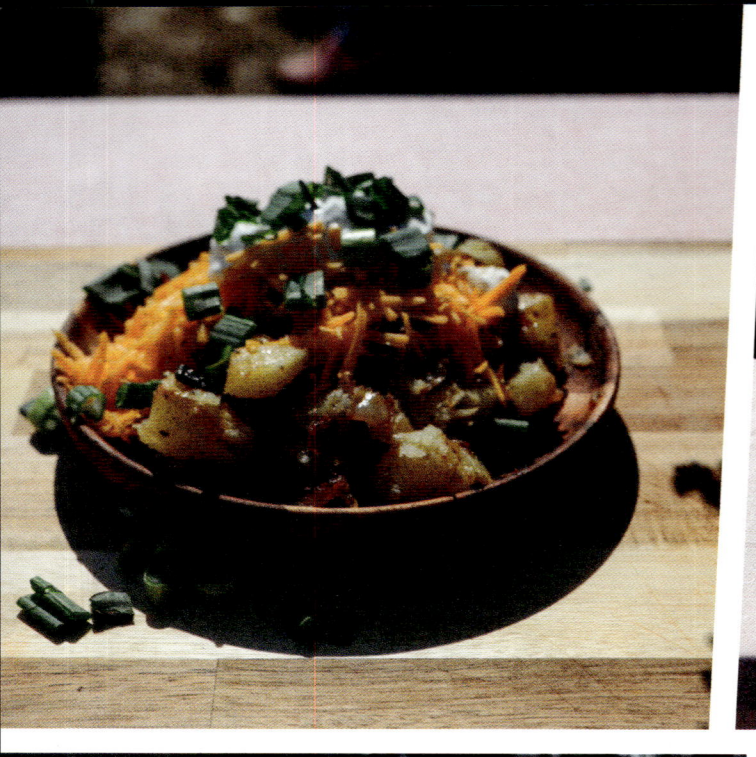

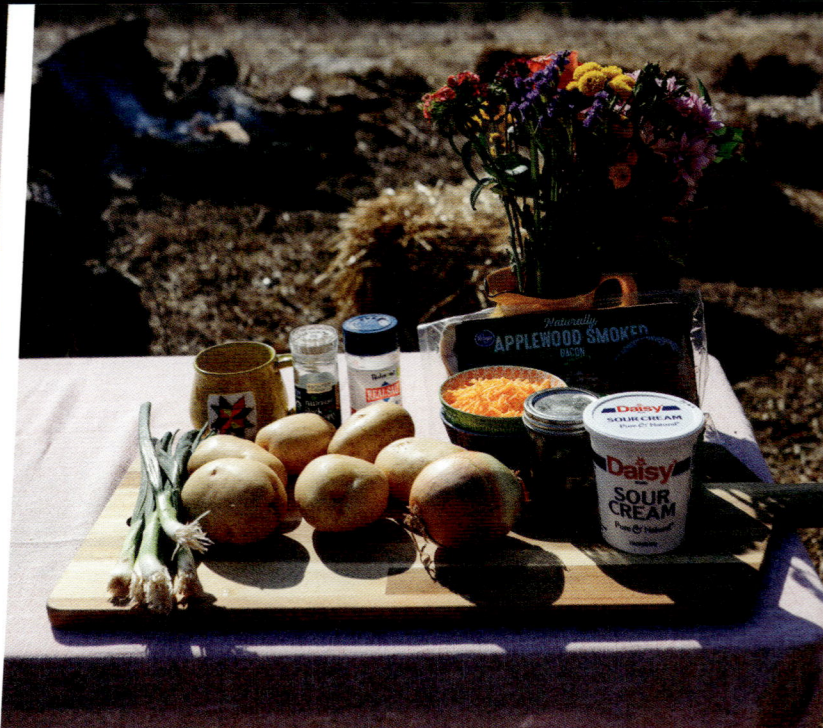

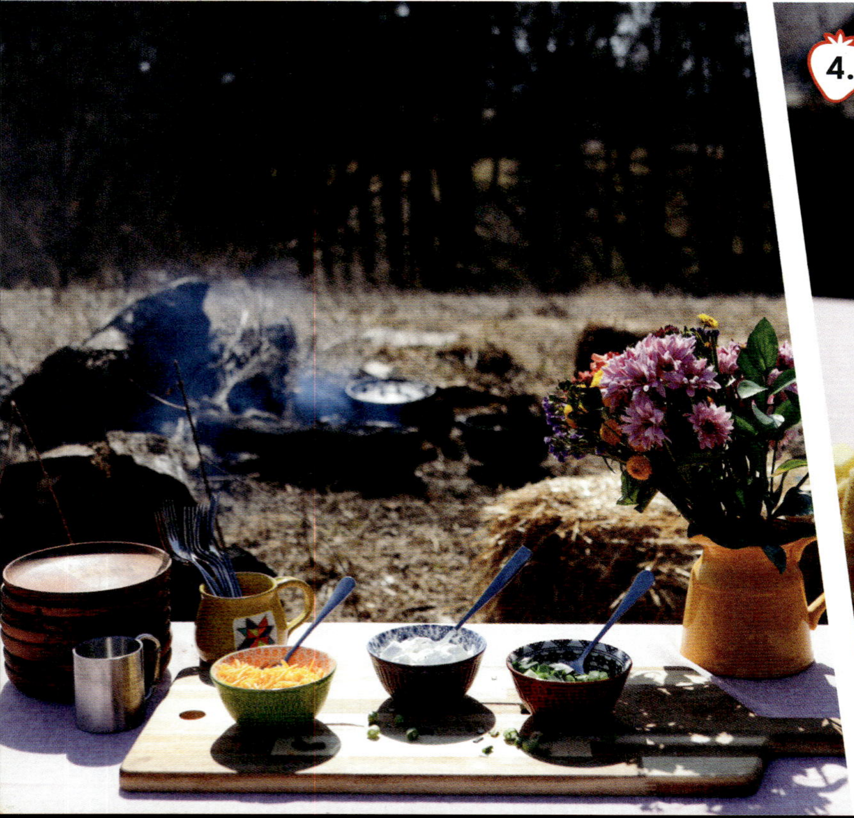

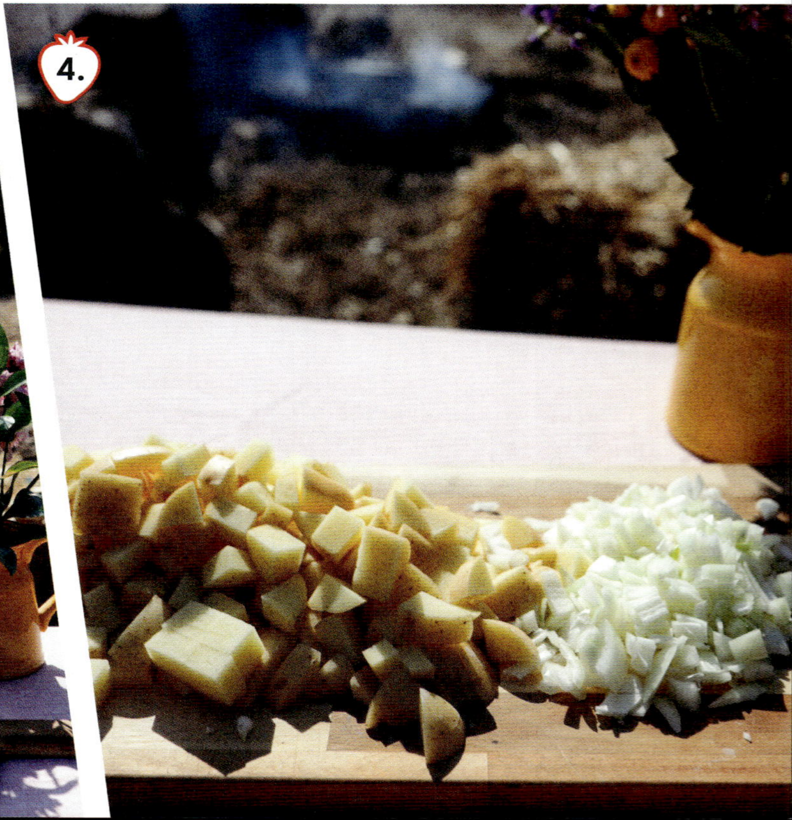
4.

Dutch Oven Campfire Potatoes

Truth be told we've made this recipe for breakfast. We've made it for lunch. We've made it for dinner. We've even made it for parties and it's always a huge hit. There aren't ever any leftovers and we're left to wonder if maybe we should invest in one more campfire Dutch oven.

TIME: 15 minutes to prepare, 35 minutes to cook
Feeds four to six

INGREDIENTS:

2 Tablespoons olive oil

6 bacon strips

6 large potatoes, cut into one-inch cubes

1 medium onion, diced

1 teaspoon salt

½ teaspoon ground pepper

2 cups shredded cheddar or Monterey Jack cheese

Optional toppings:
Diced green onions, sour cream, butter

COOKING INSTRUCTIONS:

1. Heat oil in the Dutch oven for a few minutes until hot.

2. Add bacon and fry until crispy.

3. Remove the bacon and set aside to cool and drain.

4. Without draining your Dutch oven, place potatoes and onion in the Dutch oven. Add salt and pepper.

5. Cook with coals on top of the lid and underneath the oven for about 20 - 25 minutes until the potatoes are tender and you can easily slide a fork through them.

6. Serve with crumbled bacon and desired toppings.

6.

Kitchen Sink Foil Packets

This can be whatever you want it to be! If you're serving a crowd, you can break out a bunch of bowls and fill them with all sorts of meat and vegetable options to choose from. Then you wrap it up like a package and in less than 30 minutes you'll have a filling and delicious personalized meal ready to go.

TIME: 10 minutes to prepare, 30 minutes to cook

MEAT INGREDIENT IDEAS:

*Cubed chicken breast, pork chop, or steak

*Sliced kielbasa, polish sausage, or bratwurst

*Peeled shrimp or scallops

*A piece of fish

VEGETABLE INGREDIENT IDEAS:

Onions, potatoes, carrots, garlic cloves, whole kernel corn, apple slices, lemon slices, zucchini, squash, broccoli, tri-colored bell peppers, tomatoes, mushrooms, cauliflower, beets, instant rice, pineapple, frozen mixed vegetables

SEASONING IDEAS:

Salt, pepper, seasoned salt, garlic powder, taco seasoning, lemon-pepper, cajun seasoning

Also needed:
Aluminum foil, cooking spray, 1 Tablespoon of butter per packet

COOKING INSTRUCTIONS:

1. Cut two 18" pieces of aluminum foil and stack them on top of each other. Spray the top piece lightly with cooking spray.

2. Pile in your favorite ingredients putting the meat on the top so that it's easier to check the temperature and see if it is fully cooked through.

3. Add butter and seasonings on the very top.

4. Wrap it all up in the foil, leaving some space for steam and seal it well.

5. Place your foil packet in the hot coals for about 15 minutes and then turn it over. Cook for another 15 minutes until meat is fully cooked and vegetables are soft and tender.

Loch Ness Lasagna

Not only is this lasagna easy and delicious, it's also a 'monster' in size and will feed a hungry crowd. Using frozen ravioli and your favorite jarred sauce makes prep time a breeze. Once this dish is cooking, you can just relax… or search for Nessie… Either way, this lasagna is a legend and that's no myth!

TIME: 20 minutes to prepare, 1 hour to cook
Feeds eight to twelve

INGREDIENTS:

*1 tablespoon olive oil

*1 pound ground mild Italian sausage

*½ pound ground beef

*2 teaspoons minced garlic (from the jar is fine)

*1 teaspoon italian seasoning

*½ teaspoon salt

*½ teaspoon pepper

*2 teaspoons dried parsley flakes

*2 bags (24 oz each) frozen cheese ravioli thawed

*1 (24) marinara sauce (such as RAO'S)

*1 (14 oz) can diced tomatoes and italian seasonings

*4 cups shredded mozzarella cheese

COOKING INSTRUCTIONS:

1. Heat a 12" dutch oven over 27 coals.

2. Add olive oil to the bottom and then the sausage and ground beef. Add in the salt, pepper, and Italian seasoning. Toward the end of the cooking when the meat is beginning to brown, add in the minced garlic.

3. Remove meat from the pan and set aside in a bowl.

4. Add about a cup of the marinara sauce to the bottom of the dutch oven.

5. Put one bag of ravioli over the pasta sauce and then layer on half of the meat mixture.

6. Pour the can of tomatoes over the meat mixture and then pour the second bag of ravioli on top of the tomatoes.

7. Put the other half of the meat mixture on next followed by the remaining pasta sauce.

8. Bake for 45 minutes using 18 coals on the top of the lid and 9 briquettes under the dutch oven. After cooking, remove the lid and add the cheese. Replace the lid and bake for about 15 more minutes or until the cheese is melted. Sprinkle the parsley on top. Enjoy!

Make Ahead Mac & Cheese with Veggies Please

This is a great meal to have stashed in your cooler during your travels to that first day at the campsite. There's always a million things to do when you arrive, but dinner won't be one of them if you have this make ahead marvel up your sleeve! Once the fire is ready, dinner won't be far behind. Enjoy!

TIME: 20 minutes to prepare, 20 minutes to cook
Feeds four to six

INGREDIENTS:

*1 (7 oz) package elbow noodles cooked and drained

*1/2 cup heavy cream

*½ cup sour cream

*3 tablespoons melted butter

*1 teaspoon garlic powder

*1 teaspoon onion powder

*1 teaspoon paprika

*1 cup grated sharp cheddar cheese

*1 cup grated parmesan cheese

*½ cup grated gruyere cheese

*1 teaspoon salt

*½ teaspoon pepper

*2 cups frozen mixed veggies

*2 cups crushed potato chips

COOKING INSTRUCTIONS:

1. Place cooked and drained noodles into a large bowl and add all ingredients except the potato chips.

2. Stir well to combine and then place into a greased 9x13 disposable foil pan.

3. Distribute the crushed chips evenly over the top.

4. Spray a piece of tin foil with cooking spray and place it (sprayed side down) over the top of the pan.

5. Refrigerate until ready to travel and keep in a cooler until ready to heat.

6. To cook at the campsite: Place the covered pan on the campfire grate above hot coals. Heat for about 20 minutes or until hot, melty, and bubbly.

3.

6.

Chicky Stickys

Who doesn't love the simple flavors of grilled chicken and veggies that only the char of a campfire can give? Kids love to watch these easy skewers sizzle and smoke as they wait with great anticipation to sample their handiwork. After a long day of adventuring, this is just the ticket to an evening around the fire, eating something delicious together.

TIME: 15 minutes to prepare, 20 minutes to cook
Feeds six

INGREDIENTS:

*4 boneless, skinless, chicken breasts cut into 1" chunks

*2 medium zucchini cut into ½" slices

*2 red bell peppers cut into 1" squares

*1 large sweet onion cut into chunks

*1 cup prepared teriyaki sauce

*1 teaspoon garlic powder

*½ teaspoon onion powder

*½ teaspoon black pepper

*½ teaspoon smoked paprika

*½ teaspoon salt

COOKING INSTRUCTIONS:

1. In a large ziplock bag, combine the chicken and veggies and ¾ cup of the teriyaki sauce.(Hold ¼ cup back for basting the kabobs on the grill.) Marinate the chicken and veggies for 30 minutes in the bag. It is best to do this in the fridge if you have one, or in a cooler with ice.

2. In a small bowl combine the garlic powder, onion powder, black pepper, salt, and smoked paprika.

3. Remove the chicken and veggies and thread them onto long metal skewers. Sprinkle all the skewers with the dry seasoning mix.

4. Place the skewers on a hot grate and cook them for about 20 minutes or until the chicken is done. Baste with reserved teriyaki sauce while cooking but let them get a nice char on them without basting for the last 5 minutes or so.

*You can eat these on their own or serve with ready made rice such as Uncle Ben's. This rice can be heated in a skillet over the fire. Just follow the package directions.

Chili Pie Under The Sky

This camp classic combines those two favorites, chili and cornbread, into one delicious pie! You may feel like you're dreaming but this one will wake up your taste buds in no time. The hardest part of this recipe is waiting for it to cook! …unless you forget your can opener… then the hardest part would definitely be opening the cans. Go put it in the car right now! You don't want to miss this one!

TIME: 15 minutes to prepare, 1 hour to cook
Feeds eight

INGREDIENTS:

*2 pounds ground beef

*1 small diced onion

*2 (15 oz) cans pinto beans

*1 (15 oz) can tomato sauce

*1 (15 oz) can whole kernel corn

*2 (4 oz) cans green chiles

*1 (1 ¼ oz) chili seasoning packet

*Salt and pepper

*2 tablespoons brown sugar

*¼ cup barbecue sauce

*1 tablespoon worcestershire sauce

*1 (8 ½ oz) package Jiffy corn muffin mix

*1 egg

*⅓ cup milk

*1 cup shredded cheddar cheese

COOKING INSTRUCTIONS:

1. Season with salt and pepper and brown the ground beef and onion in a 12" Dutch oven over 25 coals.

2. Add the tomato sauce, beans, corn, green chiles, chili seasoning packet, brown sugar, barbecue sauce, and worcestershire sauce and simmer for 15 minutes.

3. In a separate bowl, mix the corn muffin mix, milk, and egg together. Pour evenly over the top of the meat mixture. Do not mix this in.

4. Using 17 coals on the lid and 8 briquettes on the bottom, cook this for approximately 30-40 minutes until the cornbread is golden brown.

5. Add the cheese on top and replace the lid until melted. Remove from the heat and let stand with the lid off for 5-10 minutes. Serve this with sour cream and chopped scallions.

4.

Campfire Vampire Chicken

This delightful dinner serves two purposes: 1. Fill up hungry tummies with food, and 2. Ward off every vampire in a 20 mile radius! How, you might ask? Well it may have something to do with the FORTY cloves of garlic you'll need to make this chicken! Lucky for you (but not for the vampires) you can buy ready peeled cloves or use a 4 oz jar of pre minced garlic. No matter how you make this dish, it will be love at first BITE! Mua ha ha!

TIME: 10 minutes to prepare, 1 hour to cook
Feeds eight to ten

INGREDIENTS:

*4 tablespoons butter

*1 tablespoon olive oil

*40 cloves of garlic peeled and smashed or 1 (4 oz) jar of pre minced garlic

*1 medium sized onion diced

*6 boneless skinless chicken breasts cut into bite sized cubes

*1 (14 oz) smoked sausage cut into rounds and then again into half moons

*3 cans (16 oz) organic chicken and wild rice soup

*1 (16 oz) bag frozen mixed soup vegetables

*3 tablespoons salt free garlic herb seasoning blend (such as Mrs. Dash)

*Water *see method instructions

*½ cup heavy cream

*Salt and pepper

COOKING INSTRUCTIONS:

1. In a 12" dutch oven, melt the butter and olive oil. Add the diced onion and the garlic and saute for about 1 minute. Do not let the garlic burn.

2. Add the chicken, sausage, cans of soup, frozen veggies, salt free seasoning, a sprinkling of salt and pepper, and 1 ½ soup cans of water.

3. Using 8 briquettes on the bottom and 17 coals on the lid, cook this mixture for approximately 1 hour or until the chicken is cooked through.

4. Add the heavy cream and taste to adjust seasonings with salt and pepper.

Ready, Steady, Camp Spaghetti!

Everyone in your troop will enjoy this one pot wonder! You'll have supper on the picnic table in no time when you try this out. In fact, you may start making it this way at home too! Anywhere you decide to enjoy this pasta will be the right place and the right time. We guarantee it's a "Winner, winner, spaghetti dinner!"

TIME: 15 minutes to prepare, 20 minutes to cook
Feeds eight to ten

INGREDIENTS:

*1 pound ground beef or turkey

*2 teaspoons minced garlic

*1 medium onion diced

*1 tablespoon olive oil

*2 teaspoons dried italian seasoning

*1 (32 oz) jar spaghetti sauce

*1 (28 oz) can crushed tomatoes

*2 teaspoons sugar

*Salt and pepper

*16 oz spaghetti noodles broken in half

*1 cup water

'COOKING INSTRUCTIONS:

1. In a 12" dutch oven set on a grate, heat olive oil. Add the ground beef or turkey and the onion. Season well with salt and pepper and saute until browned. Add the garlic and saute for about 30 seconds with the meat.

2. Add the spaghetti sauce, crushed tomatoes, Italian seasoning, sugar, and water. Bring to a boil. Add in the spaghetti. Cover and cook for about 10 minutes or until the spaghetti is cooked through. Taste to adjust seasonings with salt and pepper. Serve with parmesan cheese.

SNACKS

"EVERYONE I KNOW IS LOOKING FOR SOLACE, HOPE AND A TASTY SNACK."
-MAIRA KALMANS

If there's one common denominator that exists with children of nearly all ages, it is the incessant, constant and near-unquenchable desire for, you guessed it, snacks. But if we're honest with ourselves, don't we all love a good snack from time to time? And there's something especially satisfying about a snack that you didn't just pop open a box or bag to devour, but instead took time to make outside over the fire for you and your crew. So in the spirit of snacking, here are three of our favorite, yet easiest, outdoor snacks, some with variations, that are perfect to involve the kids in at any time of day. Snack on!

> "The fire is the main comfort of the camp, whether in summer or winter."
> -Henry David Thoreau

5.

6.

Bannock Bread on a Stick

Food on a stick?! It's just plain fun. From the hunt for the perfect stick, to kneading the dough, to wrapping it like a snake coiled around your stick, to that first warm bite, it's an exciting experience that everyone can get involved in. Look for a stick that's at least 2" in diameter and is at least several feet long so you'll be able

TIME: 10 minutes to prepare, 10 minutes to cook
Feeds one to two

INGREDIENTS:

*1 cup flour plus ½ extra to ensure the right consistency

*½ cup water or milk

*1 teaspoon baking powder

*¼ teaspoon salt

OPTIONAL ADD-INS:
One egg, 1 Tablespoon of sugar, 1 Tablespoon of melted butter, flavorings such as berries, nuts or raisins

OPTIONAL TOPPINGS:
Melted butter, cinnamon sugar, chocolate sauce

COOKING INSTRUCTIONS:

1. In a large, strong plastic bag mix your dry ingredients together.

2. Once your fire is built, add your liquid ingredients and knead in the bag or on a table until the dough is no longer sticky to the touch. If your dough is too sticky, add a little more flour. If it is too stiff, add a little more liquid.

3. Add anything extra you want to add to your bread and knead until evenly distributed.

4. Split the dough into two or three even pieces.

5. Roll each piece into a long cylinder like a snake and wrap it several times around your stick, pressing slightly to make sure it doesn't fall off.

6. Bake carefully over the fire, turning often to ensure your bread cooks evenly.

7. Carefully remove and add toppings if desired.

Campfire Popcorn

Get ready for a campfire explosion - a safe and exciting explosion! This is an inexpensive and easy snack to feed to a bunch of children. It would be perfect for a daycare, a classroom, or for a party. The aluminum tray becomes the serving dish and the popcorn can be enjoyed almost immediately after it has popped.

TIME: 5 minutes to prepare, 5 - 7 minutes to pop

Feeds four

INGREDIENTS:

*1 cup of popcorn kernels

*4 Tablespoons of vegetable oil

*4 Tablespoons of butter, melted (you can melt your butter in a tin cup around the outer edge of the fire)

*Salt to taste

*M&M candies, optional

Also needed: Four 8-inch aluminum pie plates, long-handled metal tongs, heavy-duty aluminum foil, stapler

COOKING INSTRUCTIONS:

1. Fill the aluminum pie plate with ¼ cup of popcorn kernels and 1 Tablespoon of vegetable oil.

2. Cover the top of the plate with a sheet of heavy-duty aluminum foil. Don't pull it too tight. There needs to be several inches of space to allow for the popcorn to pop. Staple evenly around the edges of foil in at least five places.

3. Using your tongs, grip the pan as close to the edge as possible and hold it over hot coals until the popcorn starts popping. It usually takes about five minutes. Once the popping starts, gently shake the pan back and forth until the popping stops. It will take about three to five minutes for it to be done. Pull your pan out of the heat sooner rather than later to avoid burning.

4. Carefully poke a hole in the foil with a stick to release steam. Then remove the foil and add melted butter, salt, and m&ms.

2.

4.

3.

3.

4.

6.

8.

10.

Orange Shell Delights

Baking something in the shell of an orange as opposed to a baking pan is unique and memorable! You can use this method to try out all sorts of your favorite baked goods. Imagine using several different kinds of citrus and having orange, yellow, and green shells! Whatever you use, know that the flavor from the shell will infuse a unique flavor into what you're baking.

Orange Shell Muffins:

TIME: 10 minutes to prepare, 30 - 45 minutes to cook. Feeds four to six

INGREDIENTS:
*Three large navel oranges
*Muffin mix plus whatever additions are needed to make the mix (i.e. milk, water)

Also needed: Aluminum foil, cooking spray, mixing bowl, paring knife, fork, spoon, cooking grate (optional)

COOKING INSTRUCTIONS:

1. Prepare your fire ahead of time so that you'll have a hot bed of coals ready.

2. Prepare your muffin mix according to the instructions on your package or make your own mix from scratch.

3. You will need hollowed out orange shells for this recipe. There are two ways you can do this. The first way is to score around the middle of the orange with a paring knife without cutting all the way through. Once you've gone all the way around you can set your knife down and slide your thumb in between the flesh of the orange and the rind on one half of the orange. Gently move your thumb all the way around until you can pull the entire rind off the end. Be careful that you don't remove the little cap on the end of the orange. If there is a hole in your rind, the mix will leak through.

You can also hollow out your orange rind by slicing it in half and then carving out the inside with a spoon, similar to how you would carve a pumpkin.

4. Fill the orange rind halves with muffin mix. Leave an inch of space at the top of the rind to allow for expansion.

5. Cover the top of the orange with a piece of aluminum foil that you've sprayed with cooking spray.

6. Wrap the foil all the way around the orange.

7. Poke some holes in the top of the foil with your fork to allow some air to escape.

8. Your orange-ring muffins are ready to cook! If you're not in a hurry you can set them on a grate over a fire. This method might take up to an hour. For a faster bake, you can place your foil-wrapped oranges right into the bed of hot coals.

9. Keep an eye on the top of your oranges. You will start to see your muffin mix seep through the holes of your aluminum foil. Once the batter that's come through the top is fully cooked, you'll know that the inside of your batter will be finished as well.

10. Carefully remove your oranges from the fire and unwrap them using oven mitts. They will stay piping hot for about 10 minutes and then they will be the perfect temperature for little hands to hold so time your muffins accordingly.

Cinnamon Roll and Cornbread Variations:

Instead of a muffin mix you can also fill your orange shell with a cinnamon roll (make from scratch or pre-buy a package) or cornbread mix. It will taste a little orange-y so keep that in mind when determining what to fill your orange shell with! A Belgian-chocolate-salted-caramel-orange brownie anyone?

5 min

The Fizzy Grizzly

Everyone knows that bears love honey, but I'll have you know there's one thing they love even more. Chocolate milk! Well, old fashioned egg creams to be exact. Don't worry, there aren't any eggs in egg creams. It's just a special name for this fancy and fizzy chocolate dessert drink. Many years ago in the 1950's this drink was very popular at old time soda fountains. It's a mystery how bears came to love them so much but take caution when enjoying these in bear country nonetheless!

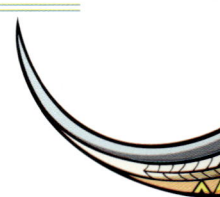

TIME: 5 minutes to prepare
Serves 4

INGREDIENTS:

*1 cup whole milk (divided into 1/4 cups per glass)

*12 tablespoons chocolate syrup (3 tablespoons per glass)

*Chilled plain sparkling water (3-4 cans)

*You will need 4 tall glasses and straws

INSTRUCTIONS:

1. Pour ¼ cup milk into each glass.

2. Add 3 tablespoons of chocolate syrup to each glass.

3. Pour chilled sparkling water into each glass leaving some room at the top (about 4-5 ounces depending on the size of your glass)

4. Stir the ingredients together with a spoon until combined. Add another splash of sparkling water on top. Enjoy with a straw!

4.

5.

6.

Muffin Cuppa Cocoa

Time: 20/25 min

This is a make-ahead at home treat that's perfect to bring with you to your campsite. Kids will love creating their own hot cocoa sticks to enjoy around the evening campfire. Using a mini muffin tin makes each treat fully customizable and that is something that kids and grown ups both will love. You could let each family member make their own row of 4 or even more if you decide to save some to enjoy at home too. These also make great gifts for friends for the holidays! Once these are removed from the tin, they can be stored at room temperature. If you're cold weather camping, that will be fine but if your weather is warm, you should keep these in your cooler.

TIME: 20 minutes to prepare, 20-30 minutes to cook
Makes 24 pieces

INGREDIENTS:

*4 cups milk chocolate chips

*2 whole vanilla beans (do not use vanilla extract)

*Your favorite add ins such as:
-Mini marshmallows
-Sprinkles
-Crushed peppermint candies
-Toffee bits
-Cinnamon chips
-Chopped peanut butter cups
-Chopped malted milk balls

Special Equipment
-Mini Muffin Tray
-Wooden popsicle sticks
 -Freezer
-Clear treat bags and twine or ziplock bags

INSTRUCTIONS:

1. Melt chocolate in the microwave in 30 second increments, stirring in between each. If you don't have a microwave, melt the chocolate in a double boiler on your stovetop. (Place chocolate in a heat proof bowl and set the bowl on top of a pot of gently simmering water. Ensure the bottom of the bowl isn't touching the water)

2. Split the two vanilla beans and scrape out the vanilla caviar with the back of your knife and add it into the melted chocolate. Stir to combine. Do not use vanilla extract because it will cause the chocolate to seize. If you don't have vanilla beans, feel free to omit this ingredient. It will still be delicious!

3. Spoon the melted chocolate into the muffin cups (no need to spray them).

4. Add your toppings.

5. Once the toppings are added, place a stick into the center of each muffin cup and freeze for 20-30 minutes until the chocolate is set.

6. Remove the chocolate pieces from the cups and store. You can place these in individual treat bags and tie up with twine or ribbon. You can also put them into ziplock bags.

To make hot cocoa:
Heat milk in a pot or heat-safe kettle on a grate over the fire. Pour 6 ounces of hot milk into mugs. Place the cocoa sticks in the mugs and stir. After a few minutes the chocolate will melt. Enjoy!

Michigan Mulled Cider

My home state of Michigan is in the top five apple producing states in the country! This means we Michiganders know a thing or two or three about apples. 1. They are delicious. 2. They make delicious cider. 3. Apple cider is even more delicious when mulling spices are added. This is a handy little mulling spice mix that you can keep in a mason jar. Make it at home and then add a tablespoon to mugs of hot apple cider around the campfire.

TIME: 5 minutes to prepare
Makes 16 servings

INGREDIENTS:

*2 cups soft brown sugar

*1 tablespoon white sugar

*1 tablespoon cinnamon

*½ tablespoon nutmeg

*1 teaspoon allspice

*1 teaspoon cloves

*1 teaspoon ginger

INSTRUCTIONS:

Combine all ingredients and store in a mason jar. Add one tablespoon to 6-8 ounces of hot apple cider.

4.

I Want S'more Skillet

S'mores are synonymous with camping. I think we can all agree on that. I think we can also agree that while they are delicious, they can be a little bit tricky for kids to manage. Here's where the skillet version comes in very handy! The skillet is very hot so you will still need to assist the littlest ones but this way is much easier than the original and just as much fun to eat.

TIME: 5 minutes to prepare, approximately 10-15 minutes to cook
Serves four to six

INGREDIENTS:

*1 bag mini marshmallows

*3 chocolate bars such as Hershey's broken into squares

*1 box of graham crackers

INSTRUCTIONS:

1. Spray an 8" skillet well with nonstick spray.

2. Place a layer of marshmallows to cover the bottom.

3. Place the chocolate pieces on top of the marshmallows.

4. Place another layer of marshmallows on top letting some of the chocolate pieces peek through.

5. Place on a grate over the fire and heat until marshmallows are melted. If you have a lid that will fit your skillet, placing that on top can help melt things a bit faster.

6. Enjoy with graham crackers!

*For another variation, try using mini chocolate peanut butter cups in place of the plain chocolate bars for a Fluffernutter S'more Skillet!

Go Nuts for Camp Donuts!

Is there anything better than a hot fresh donut? How about a hot fresh donut covered in cinnamon sugar? Ok… how about a hot fresh donut covered in cinnamon sugar that you can eat outside around the campfire with all the people you love most in the whole wide world?! Look no further, my friend. Everyone at your site will "go nuts for camp donuts!" I guarantee it.

TIME: 15 minutes to prepare, 6 minutes to cook
Serves four to six

INGREDIENTS:

*1 can butter flavor buttermilk refrigerated biscuits (8 biscuits)

*Vegetable oil for frying

*Cinnamon sugar (you can buy this ready made or make your own)

INSTRUCTIONS:

1. Place a large skillet on a cooking grate over the fire. Fill up ⅓ of the skillet with vegetable oil.

2. Open the biscuits and have the children cut the hole in the middle of each biscuit using a 1" round cookie cutter or a donut cutter. Both are available online.

3. Using a candy thermometer, ensure that the oil is at 350 degrees. Fry the donuts 2-3 minutes on each side until nicely golden.

4. Remove hot donuts from the oil and drain on a cookie sheet lined with paper towels.

5. Once drained, put a few spoonfuls of cinnamon sugar into brown paper lunch bags and let the children shake the donuts up inside until well coated.

6. Enjoy the donuts carefully. They will be hot! You can also fry up the donut holes as well and add them to the bags for coating. Double and triple this recipe as needed!

Foragers Fruit Salad

Foraging for food can be a lot of fun and can even turn into a fascinating hobby. Some of the easiest foods to forage are fruits and berries. If you know what to look for and you happen to find edible fruits and berries on your hike, feel free to add them to this fruit salad. Anything goes! The good news is that even if you don't find anything edible, you can still make this amazing fruit salad. There's always next time!

TIME: 15 minutes to prepare, 15 minutes to cook
Serves eight to ten

INGREDIENTS:

*6 oz container of raspberries

*6 oz container of blackberries

*1 pint container of blueberries

*12 oz container sliced strawberries

*2 cups grapes halved lengthwise

*1 (15 oz) can mandarin oranges in light syrup undrained

*2 sliced bananas

*Zest and juice of one lime

*¼ cup sugar

INSTRUCTIONS:

Combine all the fruits in a large bowl and add the lime zest, lime, juice, and sugar. Toss gently to combine. Let the fruit salad sit for about 15 minutes covered with foil until ready to serve.

K so... Queso?

This bubbling, warm, and flavorful dip will be a very welcome snack around your campfire. Kids and adults will love filling their bowls and dipping salty, crunchy chip after chip into this classic comfort food. Make this dish exactly one time and I assure you that you'll forever hear that age old question: K so… queso?
And I think your answer will be a resounding "Yes!"

TIME: 5 minutes to prepare, approximately 10-15 minutes to cook
Serves eight to ten

INGREDIENTS:

*1 (32 oz) block of Queso Blanco Melting Cheese such as Velveeta, cut into chunks

*1 pound ground breakfast sausage

*2 cans mild diced tomatoes,onions, and chiles such as Rotel, undrained

*2 (4 oz) cans mild green chiles, undrained

INSTRUCTIONS:

1. In a large skillet or dutch oven, cook the sausage until well browned.

2. Add the cheese, canned tomatoes, and canned chiles.

3. Cook over the fire, stirring often and being careful not to burn the cheese.

4. Remove from the heat and enjoy with tortilla chips.

THE END

GINNY YURICH

Ginny Yurich is a Michigan-based, homeschooling mama of five kids 12 years old and under and the founder of 1000 Hours Outside. She recently moved with her husband and kids to a small hobby farm and they are learning the ropes, with all sorts of new endeavors. When the stars align you might find Ginny reading or playing the piano but most of her time these days is spent hanging out with her children, and she wouldn't have it any other way.

Ginny is a thought-leader in the world of nature-based play and its benefits for children (and adults). Nature immersion changed the entire parenting journey for Ginny and she has been sharing her experiences about a lifestyle that prioritizes nature time at **www.1000HoursOutside.com.** Ginny has a BS in Mathematics and a Masters Degree in Education from the University of Michigan and she is also a speaker, author and illustrator. Her children's book, The Little Farmhouse in West Virginia was published in 2019.

The 1000 Hours Outside movement spans the globe and many people from all walks of life look to Ginny for inspiration as well as practical tips on how to put down the screens and get outside. There is a very active social media community and you can use #1000HoursOutside across social media channels like facebook and Instagram to find like-minded families who have chosen to slow down and yet gain more through nature play.

"What the child finds worthy, is worthy."
—Ginny Yurich

Meagan Nowacki is a Michigan firefighter's wife and homeschooling mom to two sons. She is the owner of The Bluebird's Nest which is a brand focused on hospitality in the Detroit Metropolitan area. She has a background in catering, baking, and event planning. Meagan has a passion for good food and good fun. She has written two cookbooks and will be releasing new books in the near future. Find her on Instagram at @ _thebluebirdsnest_ and her website thebbnest.com